FENG SHUI
DICTIONARY

FENG SHUI
DICTIONARY

EVERYTHING YOU NEED TO KNOW
TO ASSESS YOUR SPACE, FIND SOLUTIONS,
AND BRING HARMONY TO YOUR HOME

COMPREHENSIVE EXPLANATIONS
OF FENG SHUI SCHOOLS,
PRACTICES, AND TOOLS

Antonia Beattie

THUNDER BAY
P · R · E · S · S
SAN DIEGO, CALIFORNIA

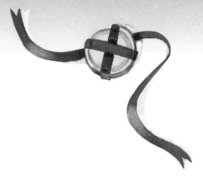

[F]or nature's truth
Is primary and her changing seasons
Correct out of a vaster reason.

—RONALD STUART THOMAS

CONTENTS

■ **Introduction 6**
  • The World of Feng Shui

■ **Some Feng Shui Rules 8**
  • The Flow of Energy
  • Yin and Yang
  • The Elements
  • The Aspirations

■ **Working with Feng Shui 16**
  • Feng Shui Tools
  • Some Simple Calculations
  • Feng Shui Schools

■ **Fixing Feng Shui Problems 24**
  • Feng Shui Cures
  • Dealing with Poison Arrows
  • Uncluttering

■ **The A-Z of Feng Shui 30**

■ **Chinese Chart of Years 184**

■ **Glossary 186**

■ **Index 188**

INTRODUCTION

The World of Feng Shui

A substantial salary, a desired promotion, and a fulfilling and interesting career are all possible if the Chinese art of placement, feng shui, is observed in your home, garden, and workplace.

The idea of an invisible life force or energy was developed in a number of ancient civilizations, including China, many centuries ago. In feng shui, this energy (known as *qi* or *chi*) has the force of the wind (*feng*), flows like water (*shui*), and is connected to every living organism. As everything is related, if there is clutter and disorganization within your home or workplace, you will similarly experience a lack of focus and confusion within your life. If you can change our environment, you can change your life.

In China, it is believed that qi can either flow or stagnate according to the shape and form of your surroundings, both natural and artificial. If it is allowed to flow at a gentle, steady pace, it brings great benefits, such as good fortune and success in business. If it is allowed to stagnate or move too fast, the energy may bring with it bankruptcy, legal worries, and poor luck.

Like wind and water, qi can be manipulated to flow beneficially using the art of feng shui, which focuses on using or blocking the energy generated by the environment around you. For example, bad

energy can be blocked simply by moving a piece of furniture in a particular direction and good energy can be stimulated by placing a few coins on a certain part of your desk.

Many of us, to some degree or other, have a feeling about what would look right in a particular room, although we may not know why. The placement of a potted palm in a certain corner may seem satisfying, even though we don't realize that the plant now shields us from a "poison arrow" created by a protruding corner.

At times, though, there may be some areas that just don't work, no matter what we do. This is where feng shui becomes particularly useful, as it can help you to identify where the qi is stagnating and choose the solution that will help qi to flow harmoniously again.

Feng shui is a very effective form of energy control because it helps us to strengthen our connection with nature. By understanding and tapping into the flow of life energy, we can link into nature's powerful balance and harmony, transforming our workplaces and homes into efficient conductors of that energy. It is not only the physical surroundings of your home, workplace, and garden that affect the flow of energy. Feng shui practitioners also believe that the name of your business, the street number of your home or business premises, and your company logo may attract or repel beneficial energy.

This dictionary will help you to understand and apply the main principles of feng shui. While there are a number of different schools of feng shui, the introductory chapters of this dictionary offer a simplified version of feng shui, giving you an understanding of the main principles.

You can then use these to explore this ancient system more deeply in the A–Z section, learning how to identify problems in the spaces around you and how to deal with them by implementing feng shui cures or clearing the clutter from your home and your life.

As you learn about feng shui, you will develop your own unique solutions for dealing with the energy flow around your home, garden, and workplace. Once you understand the flow of energy around you, you will find it easy to make a few small changes that will make a difference to the quality of your life.

SOME FENG SHUI RULES

The Flow of Energy

An invisible but powerful energy, qi, flows around and within you and all living things, and also around inanimate objects. Qi is believed to be a combination of energies generated by the shifting balances and tensions between the earth and the cosmos.

In Chinese mythology, qi is said to be created by a powerful cosmic green dragon that has its lair in a hilly terrain. All gently undulating hills are associated with the dragon's energy, and it is believed that this type of landscape, including gently flowing waters in the valleys, is a particularly auspicious form of energy.

There are three interrelated types of qi—heaven qi, earth qi, and human qi. Heaven qi is the energy of the cosmos and the movement of the clouds and wind above the earth. It is believed that the weather is caused by the various moods of the dragon; for instance, thunderstorms occur when it is feeling angry.

Earth qi is the energy generated by the shape of the Earth, the force of its magnetic fields, and the effect of the combination of the five Chinese elements—Earth, Wood, Fire, Metal, and Water (see pages 12–13). It is the energy of both the natural and artificial environments, so it includes both mountains and skyscrapers.

The best spot for a house was believed to be near (but not too near) the dragon's lair, generally halfway between the top of the hill and the valley, with the back of the house cradled by the hill. This position represents the balance between descending heaven qi and ascending earth qi.

There is also human qi, which is generated between people, as well as personal qi, which reflects the energy that moves through your body, thoughts, emotions, and personality.

It is important for the different types of qi to flow gently, freely,

and without impediment, much
like the flow of water in a slow,
meandering river. If energy is
allowed to do this, it brings
benefits to the people near it.
This beneficial qi is known as
"sheng qi."

If the energy is blocked by,
for example, too much clutter,
the energy stagnates like a river
that cannot flow freely because
it has been blocked by debris. If the qi is blocked, stagnant, or made
to move too quickly, particularly through long, straight streets
without trees lining the sidewalk, it turns into a negative form of
energy called "sha qi."

Sha qi can also be created by sharp corners, both in the shape of
a room and in prominent pieces of furniture. This form of sha qi is
called "secret arrows" or "poison arrows." They affect areas that are
at the end of a straight line—a desk at the end of a long corridor,
or a house at a T-intersection, where the road leads straight to
the building (see pages 26–27).

You will find that if you do not block a particular area from
the effect of a poison arrow, it will be virtually impossible to keep
that area free of clutter (see pages 28–29).

There are many feng shui schools of thought. However, all
feng shui practitioners agree that when qi is allowed to flow
unimpeded around the house, garden, or workplace, that area
is lucky or auspicious. An area where there is stagnation is
unlucky or inauspicious.

FENG SHUI TIP
Energy at your doorstep

Beneficial qi comes from the south and so the main entrance
of your home, garden, or business should ideally be positioned
there. However, you may wish to consider entering your home or
business through a door that faces a direction that suits your
personal qi (see "Lucky Directions and Areas" on pages 122–123).

Yin and Yang

In feng shui, as in Chinese medicine and philosophy, the life force, qi, is stimulated by the interaction between two opposing forces, yin and yang. Yin and yang are not precisely defined, but at their most basic level, yin corresponds with female, passive energy, dark colors, and the space within an interior. Yang corresponds with male, aggressive energy, light colors, and the furniture and objects in your space.

Symbolically, yin and yang are represented by the colors black and white within a circle, gently swirling around each other (see opposite). The black symbolizes yin and the white symbolizes yang. Each one contains a tiny drop of the opposing color, symbolizing that each force contains a small amount of the other.

Everything in the universe can be categorized as containing either yin or yang energies or characteristics. Yin and yang forces both attract and repel one another. This constant "struggle" between them moves qi through the universe. Once yin and yang components are in balance, the life force is in balance, which leads to a sense of well-being and prosperity in a person's life.

FENG SHUI TIP
Yin or yang?

Walk into a cluttered room or area and analyze whether there is an imbalance in the yin and yang energies in the room. You will find "yin space" rooms and areas tend to attract clutter more than other rooms. Yin space rooms often have the following characteristics:
- The color of the walls or carpet is dark, cool, gray-green, or blue.
- The area or room is overly large or overly small.
- The area or room is poorly lit.
- The area is near water pipes, where stagnation and leaking can occur.

Yin space rooms and areas include bedrooms, kitchen and bathroom cupboards, and large areas such as lofts, oversized family rooms, and open-plan areas.

In feng shui, yin and yang must be in harmony to make sure that qi flows beneficially through an interior. Yin energy is expressed by using dark gray, blue, and green colors, and in the space between pieces of furniture in the area. Yin energy is also inherent in curved walls. Yang energy is expressed with bright, warm colors and is in the furniture in the room, as well as in straight walls. It is important that there is a balance between dark and bright colors, space and furniture, and curved and straight walls.

If your home or office is too yin, you may find the space depressing and uncomfortable. To correct this, place a warmly colored cushion, seat cover, or picture in the space, and check your lighting. You may even wish to paint the walls white.

If your home or office is too yang, you may find that you feel overworked and suffer from severe headaches, accidents, and an inability to focus. Too much yang energy in a space will make you feel tired and listless, as if the energy around you has been stimulated to the breaking point. If you have too much clutter and too many bright lights and colors around you, reduce the number of books, files, and furniture in your office, and introduce cool colors and a few potted plants.

In the garden, yang energy is generated by garden structures such as decks, pergolas, garden sheds, and other small buildings, and is also found in the sunny areas of the garden. Yin energy is found in shady areas and in the space between structures and features. The front garden, a public area, represents yang energy; the back garden, a more private area, represents yin energy.

The Elements

We often think of ourselves as being very far removed from nature, especially if we live or work in a big city or town. Nevertheless, according to Chinese beliefs, we, like the rest of our world, are made up of five natural elements, which correspond to a particular direction and energy.

The year of birth indicates which element is predominant in someone's personality. See pages 56–57 to figure out your compatibility with your family, friends, and co-workers. You can also check the Chinese Chart of Years for your dominant element (see pages 184–185) and to see whether you are a yang or a yin type. The elements affect each other, and this can be productive or negative. Many energy problems in a home or office occur because there is a destructive relationship between the elements. Feng shui practitioners over the centuries have used their knowledge of the flow of creative and destructive energies to help them figure out why certain problems keep occurring in a person's home or life, and to suggest simple but effective solutions. For example, the kitchen contains the potentially destructive quality of both Water (the sink) and Fire (the stove) (see "Kitchen" on pages 116–117).

Follow the arrows of the illustration below to understand the relationship between the elements. The outer circle running clockwise indicates the creative or yang relationship between the elements—Wood helps to feed Fire, the Fire of the sun nourishes the Earth, Earth contains seams of Metal, Metal objects can be made into a receptacle for Water, and Water nourishes Wood.

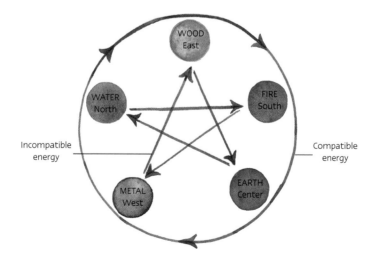

The inner five-pointed star indicates the destructive or yin relationship between the elements—Wood depletes Earth, Earth muddies Water, Water puts out Fire, Fire melts Metal, and Metal chops down Wood. The illustration opposite also gives you a solution if your home has some tense energy created by a destructive relationship between elements, such as if you have a metal statue standing next to a potted plant. Either move the statue or plant away from each other, or place a water feature between them to break the disruptive flow of energy.

Each element also "rules" the type of energy that flows in a particular part of the house. For instance, the element of Earth is considered to govern the center of the house, while Water is related to the north, Fire to the south, Wood to the east, and Metal to the west. To encourage the flow of this elemental energy in your space and life, place an item that corresponds to the energy of the element at each wall, facing the appropriate compass direction or in the center of a room. For instance, if you want to strengthen the element of Fire and the corresponding sense of creativity and forceful energy, you could add a wooden candlestick to the candle in the south of your space.

The elements also correspond to the energy of the seasons. Winter is a Water element. The next season is spring, which is a Wood element. Water nourishes wood and is part of the productive cycle. Summer is Fire, which is fed by the Wood of spring. Autumn is represented by Metal, which is contained in the Earth and can, when made into a vessel, contain Water, the element linked to winter.

In some theories, Earth represents the energy of the Chinese season of late summer, a short period of six weeks in which it is believed that the earth is experiencing a supreme balance between dark and light, life and death. Others believe that Earth does not correspond to a particular season but to the entire yearly cycle of the seasons.

ELEMENT	DIRECTION	TYPE OF ENERGY
Wood	East	Unpredictable yet exciting
Fire	South	Active and expansive
Earth	Center	Balanced and mature
Metal	West	Heavy workload with good yields
Water	North	Quiet and a tendency toward isolation

The Aspirations

In feng shui, the eight aspirations are the eight most important aspects of your life that can be affected by the flow of energy in your space. The aspirations are career, fame, health, creativity, mentors, knowledge, relationships, and wealth. Each aspiration corresponds to a compass direction (see table below).

To start the practice of feng shui, you must determine which area of your place of business or home corresponds with which aspiration. There are a number of ways of doing this, which can make the practice of feng shui seem particularly difficult and confusing (see pages 18–21 for some simple calculations).

Once you have figured out what area in your home, garden, or workplace corresponds to a particular aspiration, you can then set about remedying any problems in the flow of energy. Remedies include incorporating feng shui cures (see pages 24–25), dealing with any poison arrows directed at the area (see pages 26–27), and implementing uncluttering strategies (see pages 28–29).

However, another way of improving the flow of energy around you is to rebalance the elements (see pages 12–13). Every element—Earth, Metal, Water, Wood, and Fire—has a role to play in stimulating the flow of energy in the eight aspirations.

The table opposite suggests ways in which the elements and other objects may be used to encourage the flow of beneficial qi

around a room. This energy must be allowed to flow freely and gently through your house or business. Try not to force the energy—take some time to feel how the energy flows in your building and how the flow could be improved.

COMPASS DIRECTION	ASPIRATION
North	Career
South	Fame, acknowledgment, and promotion
East	Family and health
West	Children and creativity
Northwest	Mentors, useful friends in authority, travel
Northeast	Knowledge and study
Southwest	Relationships
Southeast	Wealth and prosperity

IMBALANCE	SYMPTOMS	CURES
Too much yin	Dark room. Feelings of depression.	Increase light. Add splashes of strong, warm colors.
Too much yang	Overcrowded room. Headaches.	Remove some of the furniture and include some dark colors in the cushions and throw rugs.
Too much clutter	Untidiness. Feeling of inability to focus or organize.	Place wind chimes over clutter.
Wealth area feels stagnant	Poor flow of money into the house.	Include a symbol of your own element in the area. Place Wooden objects or plants in the area. Avoid Metal objects. Cover all sinkholes and keep toilet lid down.
Acknowledgment area feels stagnant	Demotion or retrenchment.	Include a symbol of your own element in the area. Include plants or candles. Avoid Water objects. Do not sit with your back to the door.
Relationship area feels stagnant	Problems with marriage or other close relationship.	Include a symbol of your own element. Include red-colored objects or Wooden candle holders. Avoid Water features. Include pictures of couples or groups of two around the house.
Creativity/ children area feels stagnant	New opportunities are rare. Trouble with your children.	Include a symbol of your own element in the area. Include objects symbolizing Metal or Earth. Avoid Fire objects. Check that your back door does not open to a narrow path.
Helpful people/travel area feels stagnant	Unscrupulous people are around you.	A feeling of being stuck in one place. Include a symbol of your own element in the area. Include objects symbolizing Metal and Earth. Avoid Metal objects. Engage in a project with another person, or help a person in need.
Career area feels stagnant	Lack of opportunities for advancement in career. Feeling demoralized at work.	Include a symbol of your own element into the area. Include objects symbolizing Water and Metal. Avoid Earth objects. Clean the area and remove all clutter.
Knowledge/ education area feels stagnant	Being overlooked because of being underqualified. Inability to pass exams successfully.	Include a symbol of your own element in the area. Include objects symbolizing Water and Metal. Avoid Earth objects.
Health/family area feels stagnant	Illnesses. Feelings of tension within the family.	Include a symbol of your own element in the area. Include objects that symbolize Wood or Water. Avoid Metal objects. Clean area.

Feng Shui Tools

Two of the most important feng shui tools are your compass
and the *bagua* (sometimes referred to as the *pa-kwa,* and
explained opposite).

Your compass will help you to determine which way your
property is facing. Generally, your home, garden, or workplace faces
the most common entrance. This is the entrance through which
energy or qi enters the area.

The front garden generally faces the front boundary line. The
way the back garden faces may be harder to assess when there are
two or more entrances, especially if it also contains a garage door
opening at the back boundary line. Generally, as qi enters the
backyard through an opening or pathway from the front garden,
this area usually faces the same direction as the front garden.

To determine what compass direction your property is facing,
stand at the entrance of qi into your particular area, whether it is

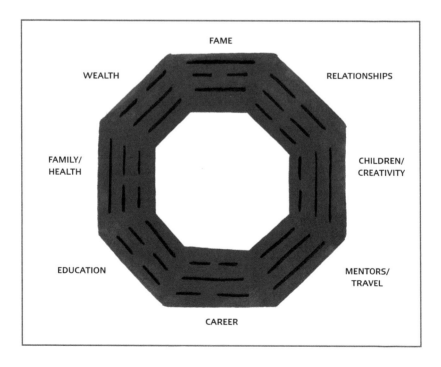

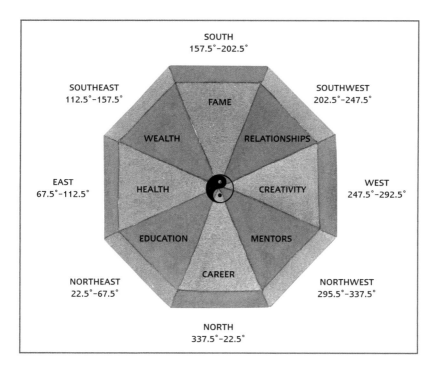

SOUTH
157.5°–202.5°

SOUTHEAST
112.5°–157.5°

FAME

SOUTHWEST
202.5°–247.5°

WEALTH

RELATIONSHIPS

EAST
67.5°–112.5°

HEALTH

CREATIVITY

WEST
247.5°–292.5°

EDUCATION

MENTORS

NORTHEAST
22.5°–67.5°

CAREER

NORTHWEST
295.5°–337.5°

NORTH
337.5°–22.5°

your front entrance, the garden gate, or the doorway leading into your office. Face the street or corridor, and note where the needle of your compass is pointing. Once you know which direction your home, garden, or workplace is facing, you can then use the bagua to figure out where the eight aspirations of life fall within your home, garden, or workplace.

The bagua is an octagonal picture or object that contains a trigram in each of its eight sides and an image of the yin/yang symbol in the center. Each trigram corresponds to a particular compass direction and aspiration area. (For more about the eight aspiration areas, see pages 14–15.) The central yin/yang symbol represents the element Earth, as this is the basis of every home or place of business.

A trigram is a "picture" of three lines stacked one upon the other (see the picture opposite). The lines of the trigram are either broken or unbroken. The broken lines correspond with yin, or introverted energy, and the unbroken lines correspond with yang, or extroverted energy.

Once you know which area of your home corresponds with which aspiration, you can then use simple ornaments, objects, and plants to increase your success in the aspiration areas of your choice. See pages 18–21 for methods of identifying aspiration areas.

Some Simple Calculations

One of the most important aspects of feng shui is figuring out which areas of your house correspond to which aspiration or enrichment: wealth, fame, relationships, health, creativity, knowledge, career, and travel. There are a number of techniques. Some use the bagua expressed in the form of a three-by-three grid, which can be aligned by taking into account either compass directions (the orientation of the building or selected area), or the position of the front door or main entrance. Other calculations require a circular template divided into eight equal segments and aligned according to the relevant compass directions.

To begin your exploration of the principles of feng shui, try the simple grid formation first. As you become more familiar with these principles, try using the bagua with compass directions. Use your intuition as to which system would best suit your house. Each system has validity and can show you how to increase the potential of your life.

The Magic Square: A Simple Grid Calculation

The *luo-shu*, or magic square, is one of the simplest ways of figuring out which areas of your home, garden, or workplace correspond to each feng shui aspiration (see pages 14–15). The luo-shu is another term for the bagua.

FENG SHUI TIP

The Bagua

The bagua is thought to signify the fundamental aspects of life, and as such is used as a powerful symbol of protection. As it is such a potent symbol, the symbol of the bagua can also be used as a powerful feng shui cure, which should only be used on the outside of a building. It is particularly effective for deflecting poison arrows created by poles, sharply angled rooflines, and straight roads. Hang the bagua (with a mirror in the center) above a door or window from where you can see a road, pole, or roofline, to deflect the negative energy emanating from these features.

The square contains a sequence of numbers, referred to as the "later heaven sequence." The formation of this number sequence is said to have been found on the back of a huge turtle. The back of the turtle's shell was divided equally into nine squares, each square containing a number of dots, ranging from one to nine. Each number came to correspond with a particular aspiration.

Follow these easy steps to find out where the different aspirations fall within your home, garden, or office, or on your desk. (Note: You do not need to worry about compass directions with this system.)

- Obtain or draw a floor plan of your building or space.
- On the plan, draw a regular square or rectangle around the perimeter of your building or space. Ignore minor projections outside this regular shape or any missing areas for this exercise; just try to make your building or space fit into a regular shape.
- On a separate piece of paper, trace the shape of your building or space and then divide it into nine roughly equal sections. Write the aspirations in the same squares as the following grid:

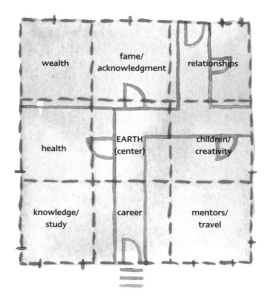

- Mark where your main entrance is and align the bottom of the grid (with the aspirations, from left to right, of knowledge/study, career, and mentors) with the wall on your plan containing your main entrance.

You will find that if your building or space is not symmetrical and there is a section missing in your plan, you may experience some difficulties in the corresponding aspiration of your life. If there is a minor protrusion (less than one third of the length of the building) in a particular aspiration, it can have the reverse effect; that is, the area may experience some benefits and good luck.

If the projection is quite substantial (for example, a room causes your building to be L-shaped), you may experience some disruptions in the aspiration area to which the projection is attached and may have to remedy the poison arrows (see pages 26–27) generated by the corner of the L.

Orientation Template: A Simple Circular Calculation

To make a template that takes into account the directions of the compass, you first need to focus on finding the center of the area you wish to assess in terms of where the eight aspirations fall.

One of the first questions you need to answer before you apply the template to your garden or property plan is whether you are focusing on your garden and home as a whole or whether you wish to analyze your house, front garden, and back garden separately.

Many Western properties do not have the luxury of a lot of space along the sides of the house. If your property has a front and back garden separated by the house and connected, if at all, by only a narrow pathway on one or both sides of the house, consider treating your front and back gardens as separate gardens.

If you are treating your house, front garden, and back garden as separate spaces, take a compass reading to find which direction your house and garden faces (see page 16), then draw a rough sketch of the house or garden. Whether the house or garden is symmetrical or not, draw either a square or rectangle around the plan. Do not worry if there are missing or slightly projecting areas within this outline shape.

Find the center of the house or yard. This can be done easily by drawing a cross connecting the four corners of the outline shape. The middle of your house or garden is where the cross lines meet.

Now, make a simplified version of the bagua (see pages 16–17) by using a sheet of transparent paper and drawing a circle large enough to span the sheet. Find the middle and divide the circle into eight equal segments. Label the segments with the names of the eight compass directions most commonly used in feng shui—north, south, east, west, northeast, northwest, southeast, and southwest. See pages 14–15 to figure out which aspirations correspond with these compass directions and write them in each segment.

Place the center of your template bagua over the point that represents the middle of your house or yard, then rotate the template so the segment of the bagua with a matching compass direction is aligned with the compass direction of the boundary line.

If you are treating your house and garden as one unit, find the center of your home by first drawing your property and within it sketching out a rough floor plan of your home. Next, draw a simplified square or rectangular outline around the floor plan and then find the middle of the house by drawing a cross running through the four corners of the outline shape.

Over this point in the house, position the bagua template so that the centers of the house and the bagua match, and the template reflects the compass direction of the front boundary line. Extend the lines, if necessary, so that the entire property (home and garden) is divided into eight segments.

Trace the internal lines of the bagua onto your floor and/or garden plan. This will give you a general indication of where the aspirations fall in your space. Make a similar template for your workplace.

FENG SHUI TIP

The fact that certain areas of your home or workplace always seem to attract clutter can indicate a corresponding problem in your life. As the clutter grows, so does your problem. If the clutter is cleared, your problem will also be cleared. This concept in feng shui stems from the idea that all forms of energy are related—if you change the energy on one level, there will be corresponding changes on other levels.

Feng Shui Schools

There are three schools of feng shui: bagua feng shui, compass feng shui, and form or landscape feng shui. Bagua feng shui involves working out a nine-square grid ("the magic square")—see pages 18–19. The eight trigrams of the bagua, which correspond to the eight aspirations of life, are thought to be the forerunners to the sixty-four trigrams used in the *I Ching* or *Book of Changes*. The *I Ching* is a poetic means of divination devised more than three thousand years ago.

The Compass School

The compass school of feng shui focuses on the relationship between you and your home, garden, or workplace, determining whether your personal orientation suits the orientation of your home or workplace. The compass school particularly concentrates on distinguishing between east and west types of people and buildings.

It is believed that if you are a west type of person, you will feel most comfortable and be most successful in a west type of home or building. If you are an east type of person, an east type of house or workplace will suit you best. A building is east or west according to its orientation (see pages 122–123).

The compass school uses a number of complex calculations as well as Chinese astrology and a special feng shui compass called the *luo-pan*. The luo-pan is a flat disk containing a Western-style compass surrounded by a series of concentric circles that identify the correspondences between a number of important aspects of feng shui, such as the elements, compass directions, and the eight aspirations.

The Form School

The form or landscape school concentrates on the flow of qi in the environment, and emphasizes the shape of the surroundings of your building and the position of your building relative to conductors of qi such as roads, rivers, and mountains (see pages 154–155). It is considered that the most auspicious position for a house and garden is midway up a mountain (representing a balance between the energies of the cosmos and earth), facing in a southerly direction with a view of a gently curving river and a small, undulating hill and backed in the north by the mountain, very much like a person reclining comfortably in an armchair with a footstool at their feet.

It is believed that each cardinal point of the compass is symbolized by one of four celestial creatures. The gently curving river and undulating hill symbolize the flow of beneficial, lucky energy, which is represented as the Celestial Red Phoenix. This energy represents a southerly energy full of good fortune, as well as the energy of summer, and flows best when you have a pleasant view or sense of openness visible from your front door or garden.

The mountains, like the backrest of a comfortable armchair, symbolize support; this supportive energy is represented in feng shui as the Celestial Black Tortoise. This energy represents a northerly, nurturing energy, as well as the energy of winter.

On the sides of the property, the Celestial White Tiger symbolizes the west and the Celestial Green Dragon symbolizes the east. The energy of the west is considered unsettled, like the energy of spring, while the energy of the east represents a time of harvest, like autumn, and the attainment of knowledge and wisdom.

FIXING FENG SHUI PROBLEMS

Feng Shui Cures

If there is a poor flow of qi within your home, garden, or workplace, sometimes the removal of old walls or the installation of a window is needed to allow the proper flow of qi. Sometimes, the entrance door will need to be changed so that it faces a different direction or built-in drawers will need to be taken out so that a bed can be placed facing the right direction for its occupant. These types of heavy-duty changes are called *rushi* cures.

However, what if you cannot afford to do any of those things or the reconstruction of part of the building is not practical? Would you need to vacate the premises? Not necessarily. You may simply need to implement *chushi* cures in your space. Chushi cures are objects that can be added to a space to improve the flow of energy there. Where rushi cures are not a practical or economical solution, chushi cures are usually equally effective substitutes.

Such feng shui cures are either easy-to-obtain objects or simple concepts that we can all use and integrate in the space around us. There are eight major types of feng shui cures:

- Color
- Reflective objects, such as lights, mirrors, and crystals
- Harmonious sounds of wind chimes and bells
- Plants and pets
- Mobiles and flags
- Statues and rocks
- Fans and flutes
- Electrical or mechanical objects

These traditional feng shui cures are the simplest ways of correcting any stagnation or fast movement of qi through your home, garden, or workplace. These cures are basically symbols that force fast-moving qi to slow down or encourage stagnant qi to move in a beneficial way. They can also be used to block harmful energy and can be manipulated to enhance the energy in a particular area of a building, such as the wealth sector. It is believed that each feng shui cure is particularly effective for a certain aspiration.

There is another level of cures, which focuses on the correspondences between the eight aspirations and the elements (see pages 12–13). Each element resonates with a particular direction and consequently with an aspiration. To enhance the circulation of qi within the area of the aspiration, objects made of the relevant element should be placed in the corresponding area and any objects made of elements that are destructive to that aspiration's element should be removed.

For example, you should place items made of wood in the wealth aspiration area of your home, garden, or workplace because the Wood element corresponds to wealth. Water also corresponds to wealth because Water nurtures Wood. However, do not place any metal in the area, as Metal can cut down Wood (old Chinese coins strung together with red thread are the exception). For the productive and destructive relationships between the elements, see the illustration on page 13.

The table below lists both elemental corrections and other traditional feng shui cures for each aspiration.

You usually only need one or two feng shui cures in order to make a difference in how your home feels and to gain some improvement in your life. Use your intuition to help you choose the right cure for you.

ASPIRATION	ELEMENTS AND FENG SHUI CURES TO ASSIST	ELEMENTS TO AVOID
Wealth	Wood, Water, plants, and pets	Metal
Acknowledgment and fame	Wood, Fire, lights, and mirrors	Water
Relationships	Wood, Fire, fans, and flutes	Water
Family and health	Wood, Water, electrical equipment	Metal
Creativity and children	Metal, Earth, solid objects, statues, and rocks	Fire
Knowledge	Water, Metal, and color	Earth
Career	Water, Metal, movement, and flags	Earth
Mentors and travel	Metal, Earth, sounds, chimes, and bells	Fire

Dealing with Poison Arrows

D ealing with poison arrows is one of the most important steps in creating a home, garden, or workplace full of harmony and balance. First, determine whether your space is being hit by poison arrows (see page 9). Then clear the clutter in that area; it is possible that the

clutter has become a type of "shield" against the negative energy of poison arrows. Never use clutter as a way of rectifying energy flow problems—all it does is stagnate energy further. However, it can be useful as an indicator that a poison arrow is present.

The following objects and environmental features create poison arrows, which may be affecting your property:

- A straight road aimed at your property
- A tree with a prominent central trunk
- A telegraph pole or flagpole
- The corners or prominent decorative lines of a building
- A straight driveway or garden bed
- A narrow corridor of property along the side of the house
- A prominent corner of a house (your own or your neighbor's)
- A prominent architectural feature of the house, such as a roofline, a column, or a balustrade, or something in the garden, such as a pergola

Inside your home or workplace, poison arrows can be created by the following interior features:

- A sharp corner on a piece of furniture
- A corner in an *L*-shaped room
- A corridor leading to an open area
- A sharp angle formed by a staircase banister

There are numerous ways of minimizing the effect of poison arrows. Many of the feng shui cures, such as water, mirrors, plants, solid objects, and objects that move, such as mobiles and wind chimes, can be used to deflect or disperse the negative energy of poison arrows.

Crystals are also an effective way of dispersing negative energy. A particularly useful multipurpose crystal that can be used in the garden is clear quartz, which must be washed thoroughly in running water before being used for any sort of work with energy. For example, place or hang the crystal over a pile of stubborn clutter to help clear the energy in the area, or hang it in a tree or shrub that has recently been pruned.

Where should a feng shui cure be placed so that it most effectively deflects poison arrows? If a poison arrow is created within your property, place the feng shui cure immediately in front of the object or feature causing the poison arrow. In a garden, plants and other garden features, such as evergreen shrubs, climbing plants, and landscaped ponds, can also be used to deflect or disperse poison arrows.

If a poison arrow is created by an object that can be moved, consider doing so—feng shui cures should be used only for features that are impractical to move. One of the reasons for restricting the number of cures you use is that too many cures can in themselves stagnate energy as their shielding energy accumulates.

Stand immediately in front of the offending feature, such as a corner, and see where the poison arrows hit. The first indication you usually get that your home or office is "under fire" from these poison arrows is an accumulation of clutter and unnecessary debris. Poison arrows travel in straight lines, and can radiate in many directions. Place a feng shui cure or a straight vertical object, such as a tassel, a crystal hanging from a piece of string, or a potted plant, immediately in front of a corner.

If the offending feature is off site (for example, across the road), place the feng shui cure between it and an important feature in your home that it is affecting, such as your front door. A bagua mirror hung above your front door is also very effective in deflecting negative energy radiating from a light pole sited directly opposite your front door.

Uncluttering

In feng shui, clutter is one of the first warning signals of an energy-flow problem in your home. Clutter and dirt block the qi that should flow freely and in graceful curves around your house and garden. Qi can bring good luck, financial rewards, and harmonious relationships if it is allowed to flow unimpeded. If the energy stagnates, bad luck and disharmony result. Any place in your home that is cluttered and dusty must be cleared.

Uncluttering is one of the best ways of reorganizing your life. However, this technique is not only about simplifying your possessions. By focusing on the details of your life, you can work out a clear path to what else you need to do or to be. By simplifying the physical clutter, you will clear the emotional clutter that has been with you since you were child and kept you from achieving your dreams.

Clutter of any form, whether it is a pile of magazines, an untidy desk full of paper, or a kitchen full of broken or unwashed pots, has a negative effect on the flow of energy in that area. Clutter can accumulate for a number of reasons. For example, clutter can have a psychological element—you may find it difficult to let go of the past or fear that you will not have enough support and protection in the future. It is important to remember that the more you let go of the past, the easier it is to attract new opportunities and positive energy now.

Try a simple experiment. Locate a cluttered area in your house. See whether a poison arrow is responsible for the clutter. Because poison arrows, by their nature, travel in straight lines, draw a straight line in your mind's eye from the object or corner generating the poison arrow to the opposite wall. Usually clutter will accumulate along the path of the poison arrow and will be

worse at the opposite wall. More often than not, clutter congregates where a poison arrow is present.

If there is no poison arrow aimed at your cluttered area, you should check whether or not there is too much space in the rest of the room. You may be making an unconscious effort to use clutter to establish a balance between yin and yang elements in a room (see pages 10–11).

Clutter also tends to accumulate in an area that relates to a particular aspiration in your life. The clutter can indicate that there is a problem within your life related to that aspiration, that an issue—and the clutter—must be cleared (see pages 14–15).

Feng shui is concerned not only with obvious clutter, but also with the hidden untidiness that can be found in cupboards, shelves and drawers, and under beds. Practitioners believe that clutter that is hidden away, particularly under beds or in the basement, indicates disguised ill health or misfortune. It is important to clear the negative energy. If you clear the clutter from these areas, you will feel a marked improvement in the area of life that the clutter was stifling.

FENG SHUI TIP
Housecleaning with luck

Feng shui practitioners use a yearly Chinese calendar that lists lucky and unlucky days. It also lists the best days for cleaning the house. However, clutter can also be cleared gradually; it is not important to clear negative energy in one go. Prioritize the areas you would like to clear; check pages 14–15 to see how a problem in your life could be solved by focusing on the clutter in one particular area.

ACKNOWLEDGMENT AND FAME ASPIRATION

To find where the acknowledgment and fame area falls in your home, garden, or workplace, see pages 18–21 for some simple calculations. Generally, the fame, acknowledgment, and promotion area corresponds to the southerly direction. This area also relates to the element of Fire.

An increase in the level of lighting in this area acts like neon lights around your name in terms of fame and acknowledgment. In

your home, leave a lamp burning (with a low-wattage lightbulb to conserve energy) in this area. In the garden, include red candles, decorative lanterns made of red glass, or pretty Christmas lights in suitable trees or shrubs.

If you sit at a desk or use a tabletop to do business with your customers, you may enhance the acknowledgment and fame area by mentally dividing the

tabletop into nine sections and placing a desk lamp in the top third of your tabletop, in the middle. This part of the desk or tabletop corresponds to the acknowledgment and fame aspiration.

Soon you will feel as if you are being noticed!

If you work at a desk or other tabletop, make sure that you are not sitting with your back to a door as this will lead to you being overlooked for promotion and can even make you vulnerable to layoff or demotion. If possible, position your tabletop so that it faces one of your lucky directions (see pages 122–123). Generally, it is thought favorable to sit facing the south or southeasterly direction to attract wealth and acknowledgment qi.

As the acknowledgment and fame aspiration corresponds to the element of Fire, place some wooden or plant-related objects in this area to enhance this aspiration. Try to avoid having any water features in this area. If you have a kitchen or bathroom in this space, hang a mirror outside the door to the room. If this room is dark, add light by means of an extra mirror, large candles, or a ventilated skylight.

If you have an entrance in this area, make sure your entrance hall is well lit and the area is uncluttered. This will encourage the entry and flow of beneficial qi. If the hallway is dark, consider a skylight. Place a doormat outside your entrance door and make sure that it incorporates the word "Welcome" and that its color scheme includes red, maroon, or orange.

If your acknowledgment and fame area is not an interior but a courtyard bounded by the walls of the building on both sides, consider installing solar-powered garden lights. If your courtyard is densely planted, be careful to keep it well pruned to let in more light. Wooden frames or gates can be backed with mirrors and attached to the walls to add interest and increase the flow of qi. Include wooden garden furniture and stain it to enhance its own natural color or choose a red mahogany stain to activate the Fire element for this aspiration. If you wish to paint your furniture, choose colors that correspond with the element of Fire.

To avoid stagnation in the corners of the courtyard and to deflect any poison arrows, place tubs of planted trees, climbers, flowers, or kitchen herbs in the corners. Choose plants, both for the interior and exterior, that do not need pruning or that will not grow too quickly. Select flowers or plants that are strongly scented, tall, and have sharp points, such as foxgloves, irises, California poppies, or dahlias. Surround the feature flower with plants that resonate with the element of Wood, such as box hedge. It is important not to neglect this area and to keep it clean, well-tended, and clear of debris.

FENG SHUI TIP

Place the image of the Imperial Dragon on the left-hand side of your desk to improve your position at work.

AMENITIES

Wealth is linked with yin energy and the element of Water. It
follows that all areas in your home and workplace that use water,
such as sinks, bathtubs, and toilets, must be in good working order
and not blocked. Also make sure that you keep all drains and plug
holes covered.

You should also take account of where such areas such as the
bathroom and kitchen are placed to prevent them from adversely
affecting your financial security and success. Figure out where your
wealth sector is both at work and at home, and see if a bathroom
or kitchen is positioned in the area (see pages 18–21).

If the bathroom is in your wealth area, you may find that money
never stays long in your household or in the business.

Another inauspicious position for these rooms is close to or
within view of the front door. At your workplace, it is equally
inauspicious if these amenities are close to or within view of the
main entrance and elevators, and it is unwise to have these
amenities positioned on the next floor directly above your main
entrance. Similarly, if you are renovating and are considering
putting in a second story, do not have your bathroom on the
second level over the entrance.

If your office faces a bathroom door, request that a screen and some plants are placed between your door and the bathroom.

If the bathrooms are inauspiciously placed, always make sure that the doors are kept closed at all times and that a mirror is placed over the outside of the doors or on them; this symbolically negates these rooms.

It is also extremely important to keep the toilet seat lid closed when not in use and have a mirror glued to the top of the lid. In feng shui, flushing the toilet with the lid up means symbolically that you are flushing away your money. If you are planning to build a house, do not put the toilet in the same room as the bathtub as this encourages overwhelming yin energy.

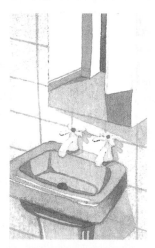

Even if the bathroom is windowless, resist leaving the doors open. If you are worried about steam and ventilation issues, see if you can have some ventilation or fans installed in these rooms and use cures such as red ribbons or wind chimes to keep the beneficial energy moving in these areas, which are usually small and cramped. If your bathroom is too dark, bring in as much light and as many bright colors as possible to balance the yin darkness and yin function of the bathroom. You may consider installing a skylight, or including a bright border of tiles or new, warmly colored towels to enliven the bathroom.

One of the most auspicious areas of a kitchen is the stove. Corporate kitchens often only contain a sink, a refrigerator, and appliances for heating food. If you do have a stove in the kitchen, it is important that it is kept as clean as possible and that it is in good working order, because the state of the stove, a Fire element, corresponds to the generation of business.

Do not extinguish this "fire" by having a Water element, such as a sink, right next to the stove. For the best luck in business and finance, it is best for the stove to face in a southeasterly direction.

ANIMAL SYMBOLS

A FENG SHUI CURE

Incorporating animal motifs in your home or office space is believed to bring the "energy" of that animal into your life (for a discussion of birds and other flying creatures, see page 43). A number of animals are believed to symbolize various beneficial aspects, such as luck, longevity, and prosperity. For example, the proper placement of a tank of goldfish attracts luck in financial matters.

In Chinese astrology, it is believed that twelve animals each epitomize a form of destiny and its related characteristics, with each animal signifying a particular Chinese year. The rat is the first animal in the twelve-year cycle—it is symbolic of cunning, charisma, and leadership. There is a belief that you can expect prosperity if you unexpectedly find a rat in your home or office.

The table below lists the twelve Chinese astrological animals, a range of corresponding years (the Chinese New Year starts later than the Western New Year—see pages 184–185), and the symbolic characteristic of each animal.

CHINESE ASTROLOGICAL ANIMAL	RANGE OF YEARS	SYMBOLIC CHARACTERISTIC
Rat	1960, 1972, 1984, 1996	Leadership
Ox	1961, 1973, 1985, 1997	Strength
Tiger	1962, 1974, 1986, 1998	Courage
Rabbit	1963, 1975, 1987, 1999	Harmony
Dragon	1964, 1976, 1988, 2000	Power
Snake	1965, 1977, 1989, 2001	Wisdom
Horse	1966, 1978, 1990, 2002	Sophistication
Sheep	1967, 1979, 1991, 2003	Abundance
Monkey	1968, 1980, 1992, 2004	Wiliness
Rooster	1969, 1981, 1993, 2005	Confidence
Dog	1970, 1982, 1994, 2006	Protection
Pig	1971, 1983, 1995, 2007	Honesty

■ FOR **ARGUMENTS**, SEE **CLEARING ARGUMENTS** ON PAGE 52.

ARTWORK

A FENG SHUI CURE

In feng shui, harmony and balance are considered to be two of the most important aspects of interior design. Artwork that is placed in a home or office to encourage luck and prosperity is usually harmonious in terms of color and subject matter.

Paintings of pleasant landscapes (and other subjects) that show skill and include flowing lines and harmonious blends of color are a desirable addition to any home and office.

Large paintings are usually placed in hallways and entrances. Large paintings and other artwork, such as statues, must always be placed in areas with a lot of space. This is not only for aesthetic reasons—it also stems from an understanding of the balance between yin (passive) and yang (aggressive) energy in a room. A piece of art, particularly if it is large or uses a lot of reds, oranges, and gold, is akin to yang energy, and requires, as balance, a lot more space (yin energy). Always choose a brightly colored piece of art for large spaces or to brighten a dark area.

Feng shui practitioners often remove scenes of battles, storms, and broken objects to improve morale in a workplace or to help in mending the relationships between family members. Pictures of turbulent water may need to be removed as well—they are thought to have a negative effect on your wealth, making your finances unstable.

It is recommended that pictures in the bedroom do not feature water scenes and placid lakes. The energy of a bedroom is yin in energy because it is designed for rest. A picture of a water scene, being also yin in energy, may unbalance the flow of qi in your personal space, and may affect your energy levels and also undermine your health.

ATTRACTING ABUNDANCE

Many feng shui cures are tailor-made to attract wealth and
prosperity to a home or business. There are two main areas that
require attention to attract a sense of abundance: the entrance
and the southeastern section of the building or garden, which
corresponds to wealth and abundance.

To attract an abundant energy through your front door, do one
of the following:

- Hang a bagua outside and above the front door.
- Place a laughing Buddha in the garden so
  that he is facing the front door.
- Place a "lucky frog" either facing the front
  door or just inside the door, facing in.
- Hang a set of solid metal rod wind chimes
  outside and above your front door.

To stimulate abundance in the southeastern
section of the building, do one of the
following things:

- Install a fish tank with healthy goldfish.
- Place a woody-stemmed potted plant in the area.
- Hang a prosperity charm (made up of a variety of prosperity
  items, such as symbols of fish, coins, small bells, jade balls, and
  red tassels) in the largest window in the area.

FENG SHUI TIP

When you are starting to unclutter a particular area in your
space, always start small. Give yourself a small uncluttering task
that you know you will be able to complete within a short time.
For example, clear the clutter from a coffee table, bookshelf, or
an untidy drawer of your study desk or dressing table. Don't try
to unclutter your whole house in one go. If you start too big a
job, you may feel overwhelmed, creating an even bigger mess
than the one you started with. When clearing your selected area,
ask yourself what is the worst thing that could happen if you
throw an item away. If the item is not necessary to you at the
moment, let it go by throwing it out or giving it away.

ATTRACTING CUSTOMERS

Two of the most effective ways of attracting customers to your business are by using exterior signs and placing advertisements effectively.

Above all, your store, as well as the signs and advertisements that you use, must be attractive to look at. Avoid decor and design that appear poorly planned. Hints of gold, expansive yang colors, and a good lighting system should be used for both your business decor and any signs. In feng shui, neon signs are considered very auspicious because the light attracts beneficial qi.

There are numerous feng shui considerations for business signs. The sign should be well proportioned, with a good balance of design elements (yang) and space (yin). It must be securely positioned, and should not cast a shadow on your main entrance or windows.

It is auspicious to use either three or five colors in the sign, symbolizing growth and balance respectively. Never incorporate a prominent image of the number four, as the Chinese word for four sounds like the word for death. Avoid triangles, which are the symbol for fire and destruction.

If you are cementing the entrance to your premises, bury six coins in the area leading to your main entrance before the cement has been poured. If you have a mat outside your main entrance, place nine coins under it to attract customers to your door.

Use curves and fluid lines in your logo and signs (see page 47). Consider also using images in your advertisements that evoke happiness, such as smiling faces and playful animals.

B

■ FOR **BALCONIES**, SEE **COURTYARDS, TERRACES, AND BALCONIES** ON PAGE 62.

BATHROOM

In feng shui, the bathroom has a yin or female energy. Because of its relationship to the element of Water, the state of your bathroom is also symbolic of your wealth. It is particularly important to keep your bathroom uncluttered.

Clear all clutter from drawers and cabinets. Separate what you do and don't need, and consider how you will store the necessary bathroom items so they are kept tidy and contained.

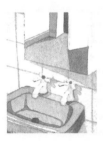

In the bathroom, clutter usually accumulates in the medicine cabinet and in the cupboards under the bathroom sink. The main clutter culprits are leftover medicines, potions, and creams that we have saved "just in case" we need them. It is more than likely that all these leftover products will have passed their expiration date before we use them again. Discard these items immediately.

Beauty products are other bathroom clutter culprits. Ask yourself how many beauty products you really need. Take note of what beauty products work for you and which you prefer. You may wish to only purchase products that have not been tested on animals, for instance. Purchase only these products and use them up, right to the very last drop. Sometimes we also manage to accumulate half-used or almost finished specialty soaps—these are made from special nurturing ingredients and essential oils, and often cost quite a lot of money. One solution is to grate all the remains and roll them into compact soap balls.

Examine your cleaning products for both the bathroom and the kitchen. Consider using only environmentally friendly cleaning products, those that have not been tested on animals and do not contain certain noxious chemicals.

Read the labels: A product may be touted as a specific cleaning agent for a particular surface but may contain predominantly the same ingredients as any other cleaning product. If so, use the product but don't buy it again—use the cleaning products you already have for other surfaces.

In reality, we only need a few products, and most cleaning agents can double up for many different types of cleaning jobs. Decide what products you wish to keep and which are most effective for your purposes, and stick to those.

Open the windows and door, wash all tiles with your favorite ecologically sound cleaner, and replace all towels and bath mats with new or freshly washed ones. If you can purchase new towels, consider buying yang-colored towels and shower and window curtains. Reds, oranges, and other warm colors will help to balance the yin function of the room.

Once the room is freshly cleaned, check the position of the toilet. In feng shui, the ideal position for the toilet is not in the bathroom at all, but in a separate room by itself. If your toilet is in the bathroom, place a wind chime in front of it to distract the attention of the energy flowing through the room.

The toilet is one of the strongest drains on beneficial energy in the home or business. Stand at the door of the bathroom. If the toilet is the first thing you see when you enter, place a flowering potted plant, such as an African violet, on the cistern, or position a statue on the floor next to the toilet. It is important always to flush with the lid down so that money—associated with the Water element—is not symbolically flushed away.

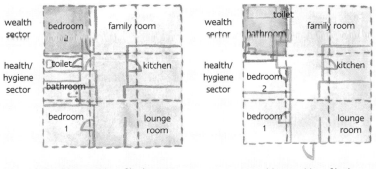

Auspicious position of bathroom/
toilet in the hygiene/health sector

Inauspicious position of bathroom/
toilet in the wealth sector

BEDROOM

One of the most important things about the bedroom is the position of the bed. It must not be placed in front of the door leading to your bedroom. This bed position is called the "coffin position" and signifies death.

From your master bedroom, you should not be able to see the toilet. The bathroom mirror should also not reflect your bed. In fact, it is inauspicious to have a mirror anywhere in your bedroom. Full-length mirrors on closet doors are considered to be particularly harmful. Feng shui practitioners believe that the spirits created by your reflection in the mirror will disturb you while you are sleeping.

Cover any mirrors in your bedroom. Having no mirrors in the bedroom, or covering up any mirrors present, is also considered an important factor for rectifying an unhappy relationship or marriage.

Keep electrical appliances to a minimum. The television should also be kept out of the bedroom because the strong yang energy conducted through the television, even when it is not on, is highly disruptive to a proper, restful sleep. If you cannot move your television, keep it covered with an attractive yin-colored cloth. Yin colors include dark greens, blues, and purples.

Clock radios are also frowned upon. Further, make sure that your electricity supply does not share the same wall as the bed, as this may cause sleep disturbances, problematic behavior, and a propensity for ill health.

Your bedroom is one of the most important areas to keep clear of clutter and disruptive energies. It is your personal sanctuary, and

---

FENG SHUI TIP

If you have a bedroom clock with a digital display, try to keep it at least three feet away from your head to reduce exposure to electromagnetic radiation. If your clock is electronic, it is best to run it on a battery rather than having it connected to the external electricity supply.

---

represents in miniature who you are and what is happening in your life. The placement of furniture, pictures, and electrical equipment can have a particularly strong effect on both your emotional life and your health.

According to feng shui principles, if you sleep poorly, clear the space under your bed. Do not have any storage there. In feng shui, having clutter under your bed means you are sleeping on all the issues you do not want to face. This will lead to many nights of disturbed sleep.

The same rules for an adult's bedroom apply to a child's bedroom. However, in feng shui, there are some special considerations. It is equally important to keep the child's bed from being positioned directly opposite the doorway, with the foot of the bed pointing toward the door. Choose a spot in the room where the child can see the door and where he or she feels snug and secure, possibly in a corner.

Determine your child's element (see pages 184–185) and favorable direction (see pages 122–123) and make sure he or she is sleeping with his or her head pointing in the right direction. This will give the child a peaceful sleep and a feeling of being nurtured. Include objects that symbolize the child's element, as well as the supportive element. For instance, if your child is an Earth element, include symbolic Earth and Fire objects or colors. Minimize  wooden objects for an Earth-element child (see pages 12–13).

If a child's window faces west, place a mobile or wind chime to minimize any disruptive energy from that direction (see page 176) and, if possible, choose a room for your child that catches the light of the morning sun.

FENG SHUI TIP

Electric blankets are not advised, as they conduct an electrical current, which can cause drowsiness and lethargy. If you must have an electric blanket, turn it off before you get into bed.

BELLS

A FENG SHUI CURE

Bells are extremely useful feng shui cures for reactivating energy in stagnant areas of a building, such as corners and dark rooms. Bells used for feng shui must make a melodious sound when struck.

A room that has a lot of clutter in it or that is full of large pieces of furniture can cause stagnant energy. This stagnant energy can give rise to a feeling of blockage in your life. Depending on where the stagnant energy lies, you may experience obstacles in your work, finances, or relationships (see pages 14–15). One of the indicators of stagnant energy, apart from the accumulation of clutter, is the tendency to have arguments or disagreements in that area.

To clear the energy in a stagnant area, simply walk into the space ringing a melodious sounding bell. Stop when you feel that the colors in the room seem clearer or the tone of the bell seems purer.

Bells are also symbolic of peace, and can be hung in the house to attract a better flow of energy. They are especially effective at the end of long corridors, where the energy has had a chance to build to a fast pace, creating a negative force.

FENG SHUI TIP

The first step to cleansing your space of unhappiness is to clear the area of all clutter. In particular, clear your bedroom totally of unnecessary objects, straighten up all your clothes, and change your sheets. Then ring a hand bell over all the areas where clutter had accumulated. Pay particular attention to your bed, ringing the bell over every inch of it. Give special focus to the pillows— this is a very useful ritual if you have marital problems, or if you or your spouse or partner are suffering from sleep problems.

BIRDS

A FENG SHUI CURE

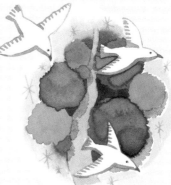

Representations of birds and other creatures that fly are often used as feng shui cures to attract love and harmony. For example, symbols of two ducks or geese represent happiness in marriage or a relationship. Birds and butterflies, especially in pairs, are also symbolic of love. Keep a butterfly carved from jade near you to attract love and romance.

To attract luck into your life, keep a symbol of a bat somewhere near you, such as at the entrance to your bedroom or work space. You may be able to find a feng shui brass bat charm that is decorated with tassels, coins, and small bells. This special "cure" can be hung in the hall near the front entrance to your home, or in the reception area of your office, to deflect negative financial energy and stimulate the flow of positive energy.

In an office, a picture of an eagle flying high above the landscape is an excellent symbol of a manager who is able to see the big picture. The head of the company would benefit from a picture of an eagle perched on black rock—this evokes a sense of far-sighted vision and a business approach that is based on strength and experience.

■ FOR **BOARDROOM MEETINGS**, SEE **MEETINGS** ON PAGE 125.

FENG SHUI TIP

Sometimes, when wishing to attract harmony and balance in your relationships, use feng shui cures in pairs—for example, the placement of two ducks on a small round mirror is a symbol of luck in relationships. Many feng shui cures involve rounded edges. When choosing a mirror, it is important to make sure that it is one that is rounded or is within a curved frame.

BOOKS AND MAGAZINES

UNCLUTTERING STRATEGIES

It is also worthwhile to look at how you deal with the clutter of books and magazines. If your work is based on gathering and using information, before you throw away anything you will need to check whether your books, magazines, and other sources of information are current and still creditable.

It is important to keep books and magazines that are necessary for your work in one place, so that you do not waste time searching for information in various parts of your home or business space.

The first step to uncluttering the books and magazines in your home is to gather them all into one area, if you can, though this may not always be possible. If you have a great number of books and magazines, try creating an area that is substantially devoted to their storage.

The next step is to sort them by subject matter or by magazine name (and date). You may find that you have an inordinate number of cookbooks. The question to ask yourself is: "How many cookbooks do I need to cook a meal?" Consider keeping only those cookbooks that fit into your current lifestyle, taste, and budget.

Donate the remainder to your local library or your favorite charitable organization. You may also wish to transcribe or copy your favorite recipes and place them in a binder.

Reference materials, such as encyclopedias, usually need to be kept up-to-date. Ask yourself whether you really need a complete set of encyclopedias that came out in 1960. There are now available a number of excellent encyclopedias online and on CD-ROM—these take up very little space on your bookshelf or desk. Do not forget that you can always donate your reference books to your local library, and go and see them there whenever you want.

You will need to decide whether to keep or discard your magazines.

Your stash of magazines may go back many years, and you may have forgotten why you chose to keep individual issues. Look at whether or not you are keeping a particular issue just for one article. If you are, simply photocopy the item and place it in a plastic insert or sleeve in a folder.

Consider donating the intact magazines to your local library or your doctor's waiting room. Review your folder yearly to see which articles—if any—you have used during that time, and then decide which should be kept and which thrown out.

Photographic magazines are often hard to let go of because of their array of pictures of usually exceptional quality. Your best solution would be again to give them to your local library or school, where they will be appreciated and used and where you can still access them whenever you want.

Once you have reorganized your books and magazines, you will feel that the flow of energy is clearer and brings with it a more positive energy.

How do you tell whether you have successfully cleared stagnant energy from your house? Here are some indications that the negative energy has been cleared. You may feel that:

- There is a lightness in the air.
- The colors in the room or house are brighter.
- Everything is in its place.
- An indefinable worry is no longer lingering around you.

FENG SHUI TIP

Susan collected all her old magazines, catalogs, and articles and used them to create a picture calendar for a preschool child. She cut out all the pictures and arranged them in groupings and gave each day a different theme. The child to whom she gave it enjoyed looking at the pictures and identifying the subjects. As well as being a functional calendar and a delightful gift, it also became a pictorial learning tool.

BUDGET AND BUSINESS IMPROVEMENT

Feng shui methods of increasing wealth for your business and profits for you and your work colleagues often involve the use of coins and water. To help you meet your budget, consider one of the following strategies:

- Place a Chinese good-luck coin in a red envelope and tape it to your checkbook.
- Place an eight-coin charm inside your checkbook.
- Keep a piece of citrine in the wealth section of your work desk or table.
- Place a pair of small figurines called "lucky cats" beside the cash register.
- Use a small figurine called Lin Hai, which carries an oversized coin and a peach, symbolizing a long and fruitful business.

If your bathroom is positioned in the wealth sector of your house or business, you will need to take extra precautions to make sure you do not lose money as soon as you make it, such as by placing a mirror on the toilet lid, on the wall behind the toilet, or on the door to the bathroom. By positioning the mirror in one or all of these places, you are creating an illusion that the toilet is not really there. Try this for one week, and see if you experience a beneficial change in your finances.

FENG SHUI TIP

North corresponds to your career aspiration. If you want a career change or improvement in your working conditions, make sure that the northern area of your house is neat, clean, and uncluttered, and include a feng shui cure, such as a melodious-sounding wind chime or a mobile hanging from the window, to enhance the flow of positive energy in that area.

BUSINESS NAMES AND LOGOS

In the Chinese business world, the auspiciousness of a company's name is determined by the number of strokes taken to write it in Chinese characters. This is not really applicable in the West; however, there are still some important feng shui principles that should be observed for Western business names.

Names chosen for a business should be appropriate and should include words with positive connotations or that are uplifting or inspiring. In China, many business names include words such as "happy" or "lucky." Be careful also with words that sound similar to negative words, such as "death," "hate," or "forgotten."

Logos are an integral part of your business and great consideration must be given to having a well-balanced and appropriate design. Designs that are considered auspicious are those that incorporate fluid, gently curving lines; these symbolize the beneficial flow of qi and are reminiscent of the sinuous lines of the dragon. The incorporation of a fat and happy dragon in a logo is especially fortunate.

Some lucky images include upright arrows. Arrows that point downward are inauspicious and should be avoided, as should crosses, as they symbolize problems and strife. If you have designed a vibrant symbol, it is inauspicious to enclose it with a circular border, as this symbolizes the constriction of energy. Otherwise, the circle is an auspicious sign, as it symbolizes heaven, and so is the square, as it symbolizes earth.

FENG SHUI TIP

Make sure there is a balance between yin and yang elements in your logo. The design should be a balance between dark and light areas, between space and lines, and between curved and straight lines. The logo should present a harmonious, balanced image.

BUSINESS SUCCESS

To encourage success in business, clear your office or workplace of clutter and dust. Once you have cleared the space, focus on removing certain objects that may be attracting bad luck to you without your realizing it. Focus on the pictures near you at work—are they harmonious and attractive? Remove any pictures of turbulent water, as water and money are closely connected in feng shui, and do not have any battle scenes in your office decor.

Avoid placing pictures of mountains directly in front of where you work, or directly in front of the entrance to your work or business space. They will create an obstructive energy that will lead you to encounter one obstacle after another in your business. Place a picture of mountains at your back—this will encourage feelings of strength and support, and is an especially effective cure if you suffer from lower back problems at work.

Pictures that encourage success in your workplace include photographs or images in any medium of animals that are related, in feng shui, to abundance, such as fish, pheasants, phoenixes, boars, or toads.

Special money charms featuring frogs are very effective for encouraging a flow of abundance to you. The feng shui Fortune Frog can be placed just inside your office door, looking into your workplace. Place him on a shelf rather than on the floor. The Fortune Frog is either three-legged or sits on a pile of gold coins. He is usually gold in color and has a slit in his mouth into which you can insert a coin.

If you use files in your work, keep a small cure of three feng shui coins tied into a package with red thread over a file that represents an important project. You can also place this simple package over any documentation or book of accounts that represents the financial status of your business.

If you work with a cash register, place the package on top of the machine and place a mirror beside it to multiply the money coming to you. Placing a bell over the register will also stimulate abundant energy.

If you sit at a desk, you can make the tabletop a miniature version of your workplace—the wealth section will correspond to the top left-hand section of your desk. Place one (and only one) of the following feng shui cures in this area to stimulate good business:

- The Fortune Frog
- A crystal ball made from citrine, a stone that resonates with abundance
- A special eight-coin charm
- A jade tree
- A flowering potted plant with red or pink flowers, such as an African violet

When planning to expand in the future, be careful to take some of the feng shui principles in this dictionary into account. Often, successful businesses that have thrived in one residence suffer due to an overextension of the business. For example, by adding an extension to a certain part of your building, you may be creating poison arrows that are directed straight to your sales team manager, in which case you may soon experience low morale issues from your sales force. Either move the sales team or consult a feng shui practitioner to make sure that you do not damage the energy flow of your business.

Extensions that are less than one third of the length of the building are usually beneficial to the aspiration to which that area of the building corresponds. For example, if you build an extension to your wealth area that is less than one third of the length of the existing building, you will probably find that your business will show improvement.

FENG SHUI TIP

If a business is expanding, it is wise not to let go of the premises that brought it luck. It is thought to be most auspicious if the lucky premises are kept and extra premises are taken nearby.

C

CAREER ASPIRATION

In feng shui, your career resonates in the northern section of your home and office. If you wish to succeed and to impress your supervisor with your work, install bright, cheerful curtains or place throw pillows made from yang-colored fabrics in your work area.

You can be overlooked if you are sitting with your back facing the entrance to your workspace. Try to reposition yourself so that you are facing the entrance, or place a mirror on your desk so that you can see the entrance while you work facing away from the door.

However, if your career feels overstimulated—if you feel you are unfocused and trying to do a hundred things at once—you may wish to rebalance the energy in this area with yin (dark-colored) fabrics or a piece of dark furniture.

This northerly section resonates with the element of Water, so remove any large objects that resonate with the element of Earth, such as large earthenware pots and leafy potted plants. As this area corresponds with the element of Water, its energy can be enhanced by placing items in it that are predominantly water-related, such as a small wall fountain, or that resonate with the energy of Metal, such as decorative brass pots or photographs in silver frames. In the productive cycle of elements, Metal sustains Water in the same way as a metal bowl holds water, giving it form.

It is very important to keep this area as free from clutter as possible. Also, remove any dried flowers from this section of both your home and your office, and be vigilant about removing fresh flowers once they start to lose their first flush of beauty and energy. Pictures of mountains that you can see as you are sitting at your desk should be repositioned to hang on the wall behind you.

career area

main entrance
to space

Clean this northerly section of your home and your portion of the workplace, clear these areas of clutter, and deal with any poison arrows (see pages 26–27). Once you have cleared the spaces, include a picture of a confident creature, such as a monkey or rooster, or place a yellow tassel on your desk to attract promotion. The image of a pagoda is also believed to signify success in business—it symbolizes your ability to rise through the hierarchies at work. Place this cure behind you so that it can strengthen your back and give you a sense of support.

Also, if you are sitting a little low in relation to your tabletop, you may find that you are missing various opportunities and being overlooked. Consider placing a small platform under your chair, which will raise you to an ergonomically acceptable level in relation to your desk. This platform is a symbol of kingship and confidence. Even if you don't feel confident at first and don't feel that you can get the job of your dreams, you will be attracting this kind of energy to yourself by sitting on your platform, and eventually you will feel able to take control of your life and aim high.

If this area is too yin (too dark), include a brightly colored cushion or increase the level of light in the area. Always keep light fittings in good order and change lightbulbs as soon as they burn out. Always keep lightbulbs covered with lamp shades or other fittings, such as Chinese rice paper lanterns.

FENG SHUI TIP

When you are applying for a job, tie a black tassel to the handle of the briefcase you will be taking with you to the interview. (You could attach the tassel to the inside of the briefcase instead.) Make sure that your briefcase is black, with a gold-colored trim. In feng shui, black symbolizes endurance and strength, while gold symbolizes wealth and prosperity. To attract luck, consider also placing six I Ching coins in the briefcase.

CLEARING ARGUMENTS

Are there too many arguments in your
family home or workplace? If so, there are
some very useful feng shui strategies you can
effectively use to lower feelings of aggression
among family members and work colleagues.

Arguments usually occur where the energy flow
of your home or office is disturbed, stagnant, or
attacked by a poison arrow. Arguments expend yang
energy and can occur as a result of too much of this
energy accumulating in one area, because of either a
poison arrow or too many pieces of furniture
cluttering the area.

During an argument, one of the hardest
tasks is listening rather than talking louder than
the others involved. You can alleviate feelings of resentment by
making sure that neither you nor other family members or work
colleagues are standing or sitting with your back to a doorway. If
you are in the living room, make sure that there is an even number
of chairs, and that you and your family are sitting in a position
where you can see the doorway. This will lead all of you to seek—
and find—solutions to your problems.

Make a note of where the arguments erupt in your home and
your workplace. Check that these areas are not at the end of a long
corridor—a spot that suffers from hard-hitting poison arrows
generated by fast-moving qi. Energy that runs fast along a corridor
negatively affects not only the corridor but also the area where the
energy hits, usually a wall that is positioned perpendicular to the
corridor. This energy also negatively affects the room or area on the
other side of the wall. Note whether the argumentative person has a
room—an office or a bedroom—at the end of a corridor. If possible,
place some protective shields in this area, otherwise that person will

literally feel constantly under attack.

At the wall where the energy hits,
place a lush, healthy-looking plant to
disperse the residual negative energy
that is leaking into the room, or hang a
picture of an eagle as a protection against
bad luck.

If the problem you are suffering from is family disruptions, a picture or other image of an animal that symbolizes peace and harmony, such as a rabbit or phoenix, is a good feng shui cure. These animals have yin qualities that will help to calm the overstimulation that an excess of yang energy can bring. Place the picture or image in the living room if you are having arguments within the family group, or in the room of the person who appears to have an excess of yang energy.

Take note as well of the subject matter of the pictures decorating the walls of your living area. Are they harmonious? Do they have pleasant associations? If not, replace the offending pictures, because they are symbolic of the current feelings of the family.

Check also that the living room is not being struck by poison arrows made by sharp lines from a neighbor's roof line. If it is, implement the solutions discussed on pages 26–27. Also, look up and check whether arguments are occurring under an exposed beam. If they are, try tying a tassel from the beam to dissipate symbolically the negative energy created by the beam.

Once you have implemented a cure, ring a melodious hand bell in the area. Constant arguments make the air of an area feel heavy, sound flat, and seem dull in color (as if the area is covered in a light layer of dust). Ring the bell over the area, particularly over upholstered pieces of furniture, until you sense a change in the air. Upholstery can soak up a lot of negative energy because it has close contact with people.

■ FOR **CLOTHES**, SEE **SHOES AND CLOTHING: UNCLUTTERING STRATEGIES** ON PAGES 156-157.
■ FOR **CLUTTER**, SEE **UNCLUTTERING** ON PAGES 160-169.

COINS

A FENG SHUI CURE

Chinese coins are often used in
feng shui to attract positive energy
for financial ventures or to stimulate the
flow of wealth and abundance into a home or
business. Chinese coins are usually replicas that are dull
gold in color; they are round with a square hole. They
vary in size and can be found made up into charms that
sometimes include other features signifying success and luck,
such as a jade bead and a red tassel.

The number of coins used is important. Package three Chinese
coins in a pile with red string and place the package on an account
book to attract money to your business. Place the package on the
top left-hand side of your desk when you are going to ask for a
promotion that involves a higher salary. Place the coins in a red
envelope and carry this with you when you ask your bank manager
for a loan.

You can also obtain a six-coin charm where the coins are
secured in a row, with a jade bead and red tassel at the end. Hang
this from the back of your chair to counter any negative energy that
is aimed at you (if your back is facing the entrance to your
workplace) or to deflect negative comments from work colleagues.

FENG SHUI TIP

If you want to enhance an aspiration in the relevant area in
your home or workplace, a simple solution is to keep a light on
in that area for at least two or three hours during the evening.
As general principles:
• Keep light fittings in good order.
• Change lightbulbs when necessary.
• Keep lightbulbs covered with lamp shades or other suitable
  fittings.

COLORS

A FENG SHUI CURE

The color of plants, ornaments, flags, lanterns, and panels of mosaics, as well as of walls, doors, and furniture in the garden, can help to stimulate the flow of energy around the garden to enhance a feeling of harmony and balance. Colors, like shapes, directions, and aspirations, correspond with the Chinese elements of Wood, Water, Earth, Fire, and Metal. The table below lists the correspondences between elements, colors, directions, and the type of energy the color generates.

In feng shui, color is used in harmony with the five elements: Earth, Water, Fire, Wood, and Metal. Over the centuries, Chinese philosophers have determined the correspondences between these elements and various other aspects of life. For instance, the element of Earth governs the center of the house, so this is a good area to include yellow, earthy, and golden-hued colors. Similarly, the element of Water governs the northern portion of the house, which may be decorated with blue hues and colors with a touch of black in them. The element of Fire rules over the southern part of the house. Decorate this area with reds and oranges. The eastern portion of your home should have some blues and greens in the color scheme to connect it with the element of Wood, while the west would benefit from being decorated with whites, creams, and silvers to encourage the energy of the element of Metal. To minimize the effect of overhead beams, paint them white (or any light color).

To stimulate qi energy in your home or office, it is a good idea to use bright yang colors, such as reds and yellows. The use of strong colors, such as red, black, and gold, invites good prosperity into the building. However, too much yang energy may be detrimental. It is important to achieve a balance between yin and yang colors (see pages 10–11).

ELEMENT	COLOR	DIRECTION	YIN/YANG
Earth	Yellow	Center	Yang
Water	Black	North	Yin
Fire	Red	South	Yang
Wood	Blue/Green	East	Yin
Metal	White	West	Yang

COMPATIBILITY

ELEMENTAL COMPATIBILITY

To check your compatibility with your partner, friends, family, or work colleagues, first identify which one of the five elements you resonate with. To figure out which element represents your personality, simply note the last digit of your year of birth. The table at right outlines the dominant element for the Chinese solar years that end in particular digits and notes whether the element is yang (aggressive) or yin (passive) in energy.

If our personalities contain the yang aspect of an element, we strongly embody that element's characteristics. We can be more assertive and energetic. Yang energy is outgoing, active, and positive. Yin energy is softer and more fluid.

LAST DIGIT	ELEMENT	YIN/YANG
1	Metal	Yin
2	Water	Yang
3	Water	Yin
4	Wood	Yang
5	Wood	Yin
6	Fire	Yang
7	Fire	Yin
8	Earth	Yang
9	Earth	Yin
0	Metal	Yang

The person who is more yin will have quite a few of the element's characteristics but may also have characteristics of some of the other elements, particularly from the supporting element and also from the destructive element (see table below). For instance, if you are a yin Water element, then you may also have characteristics of the supportive Metal element and the unsympathetic Earth element. The table at the top of page 57 gives you some of the characteristics of each element.

Next, ascertain the elemental personality of your partner, friends, and work colleagues. As each element has a particular supportive or destructive relationship with the other elements, this

ELEMENT	CONSTRUCTIVE ELEMENTS (High compatibility rating)	DESTRUCTIVE ELEMENTS (Low compatibility rating)
Earth	Earth, Fire, Metal	Wood, Water
Metal	Metal, Earth, Water	Wood, Fire
Water	Water, Metal, Wood	Fire, Earth
Wood	Wood, Water, Fire	Earth, Metal
Fire	Fire, Earth, Wood	Metal, Water

ELEMENT	PERSONAL CHARACTERISTICS
Earth	Loyal, attentive, thorough, stubborn, needy
Metal	Controlled, organized, idealistic, controlling, authoritative
Water	Resourceful, independent, imaginative, secretive, uncommunicative
Wood	Practical, open, self-starting, competitive, restless
Fire	Compassionate, communicative, intuitive, willful, lacking in detail

is echoed in the interrelations between people with particular elemental personalities. Your calculations may provide you with some startling insights on why some of your relationships seem so effortless while others seem to need a great deal of work! The table on page 56 lists which elements are either compatible or not very compatible with each other.

Where elemental personalities are in a destructive relationship with each other, try to offset some of the negative effects of the combination by consciously infusing your relationship with goodwill.

If your relationship with a work colleague is destructive, include a balancing element in the relationship area of your office or desk. For example, if you correspond to the Wood element and the person you have difficulties with corresponds to the Metal element, place a Water-element feature, such as a small bowl of water and very fresh flowers or a fish tank, in the relationship corner of your workspace.

If your relationship with a partner, friend, or family member is destructive, you can also include a balancing element in the

DIFFICULT COMBINATIONS	BALANCING ELEMENT	SUGGESTIONS FOR GIFT IDEAS
Earth and Water	Metal	Metal sculpture; jewelry
Metal and Wood	Water	Aquarium; weekend at a beach resort
Water and Fire	Wood	Large potted plants; wicker picnic basket
Wood and Earth	Fire	Fireplace; romantic scented candles
Fire and Metal	Earth	Large blue and white earthenware jars or tubs; blue and white tea set

relationship area of your home or in the bedroom. If feelings are particularly fraught, consider giving your partner, friend, or family member a present incorporating the balancing elements, as outlined in the table.

EAST/WEST COMPATIBILITY

Another way of figuring out your compatibility with others is to determine whether you and your partner, friends, or work colleagues have an east or west orientation.

Each person has either an easterly or westerly orientation. The following calculations will also help you to figure out your orientation. If you want a shortcut, see pages 184–185 for the correspondence between your year of birth and your orientation.

Be careful if your birthday falls at the beginning of the year, and check the Chinese calendar to see whether your year of birth is really the previous year by Chinese reckoning (see pages 184–185). For example, if you were born on January 5, 1965, your year of birth is 1964, because the Chinese year of 1964 ends on February 1, 1965.

Step 1: Getting the remainder

Add together the digits of the year of your birth; for example, if it is 1963, you should add 1 + 9 + 6 + 3, getting a total of 19. Divide the total by 9.

In our example, this would be 19 divided by 9, giving you a resulting number of 2 and a remainder of 1.

Step 2: Getting your orientation number

- If you are male, subtract the remainder from 11: i.e., 11 - 1 = 10. If the resultant number is higher than 9, subtract 9 from the resultant number: i.e., 10 - 9 = 1.

- If you are female, add 4 to your remainder; i.e., 1 + 4 = 5.

If you get 5 as your orientation number and you are female, change your number to 8 and, if you are male, change your number to 2. This is because 5 (the number of the Chinese elements and the middle number of the magic square) is reserved for the number symbolizing Earth.

If your calculation results in zero, use 9 as your orientation number.

Step 3: What does your orientation number mean?

If you get 1, 3, 4, or 9, your orientation is east. It follows from our example that a male person born in 1963 has an eastern orientation. If you get 2, 6, 7, or 8, your orientation is west.

From a feng shui perspective, it is strongly advised that for a long-lasting and harmonious relationship, the people should be within the same orientation group. This is recommended for married couples, as well as for relationships between parents and children.

Similarly, the most harmonious work relationships occur between people of the same orientation. If you employ staff or are a manager of a group of staff members, it would be worthwhile to figure out the elemental correspondences and east/west orientation of your work group. Make a note of who seems to get along with whom. You might be surprised by how feng shui calculations explain camaraderie between some staff members and animosity between others.

Make a note of the number that you obtained, as you will be able to figure out your lucky areas and directions (see pages 122–123). To determine your compatibility with your home and your workplace, see pages 136–137.

CONCENTRATION

IMPROVING YOUR CONCENTRATION THROUGH FENG SHUI

To improve your concentration, first clear and organize your work, notes, and assignments so that everything is in a logical place and there is space for everything you need. To encourage this form of clearing, hang a clear quartz crystal over the desk—its energy will help you to eventually clear your space.

If you are finding yourself feeling distracted or unfocused, check that the following do not apply to you:

• Your back is facing the entrance.

• You are sitting in an uncomfortable chair.

It is a common feng shui principle that you should never sit with your back to an entrance. This attracts anything from bad luck to

feelings of being disturbed in your work. Your chair must be comfortable. In feng shui, the most auspicious kind of chair is one that has armrests and a high back—this signifies the support of mountains behind you and symbolically strengthens your spine.

Similarly, hang a picture of mountains behind your chair. An image of a pagoda can also be placed behind your back in the place you work. The pagoda has a similar energy to a mountain but it symbolizes climbing through levels of expertise. To help you in the advancement of your studies, hang a yellow tassel over your desk.

Crystals are another excellent way to focus your attention (see page 66). If you are in the midst of exams or assignments are due, place a crystal in each corner of your study room. Use crystals such as tiger's eye and fluorite to help you with your studies. Tiger's eye helps to clarify your thoughts and fluorite is renowned for its ability to help you retain what you have learned.

In feng shui, sound is also considered particularly useful for stimulating beneficial energy. It is important that the sounds are melodious; think, for example, of the pleasant, random tinkle of a wind chime. However, you could also consider playing a melodious piece of music while you work. Western scientists have been experimenting for a number of years in an attempt to understand the effect of music and harmony on our minds. It has been found

that constant exposure to certain types of musical stimulation can raise our level of awareness.

As with all things, balance is the key—too much music can lead to overstimulation. In feng shui terms, the music becomes too yang or "aggressive" if it is played too loudly or if the sound is too jarring. This type of music will cloud rather than stimulate your thought processes.

If you are working to a close deadline, listening to Gregorian chants can help to lower your stress levels. The slow, tranquil rhythms will remind you to breathe more deeply into your diaphragm. This will help to relieve stress, because anxiety and panic are often closely related to shallow breathing or hyperventilation. To keep a clear head while working, consider listening to some Mozart, Bach, Vivaldi, or Haydn.

Always remember to clear the space at the end of each project, and if possible, file the information in the knowledge area of your home or office. By taking this information out of your study area, you are symbolically indicating that you wish to move forward with your studies. However, as you are still keeping the necessary files in the knowledge area of your home or workplace, you are retaining the information that you will need in order to continue your studies successfully.

FENG SHUI TIP

Here are some stones that are believed to help aid concentration and memory:

- Agate
- Amethyst
- Aquamarine
- Cat's Eye
- Emerald
- Onyx

One of these stones can be placed on your worktable in an area that corresponds with your knowledge or creativity aspirations, or stroked periodically. These strategies can noticeably assist concentration.

COURTYARDS, TERRACES, AND BALCONIES

COURTYARDS

Courtyards offer the opportunity, in feng shui terms, of expanding your house space to make it regular in shape, so that beneficial energy can flow auspiciously around your property and life. The courtyard area also gives you the opportunity to create a private "garden room" that extends your living areas and brings more of the garden's beauty and energy into your life.

Courtyards are often situated at the back of the house. This is a yin energy area, and you can easily make the space a lovely private oasis where you can regain your composure and relax after a stressful day. The right amount of yin energy invites a quieter, more contemplative mood; make sure this area does not become overgrown, cluttered, or too shady.

If the space is too sunny, add a large umbrella covered with fabric that is either a natural white or a yin color such as blue or green. If the energy is too yin, incorporate a yang element, such as Christmas lights encircling the entire space. Also consider installing an upward-pointing light facing south to stimulate the flow of lucky energy.

As courtyards tend to be small, another way of encouraging energy to flow around the space is to use gentle sounds that travel well by bouncing off the courtyard walls and fence. Incorporate wall fountains facing north or east, or metal wind chimes facing west.

TERRACES

Terraces are an excellent way of dealing with sloping land. Feng shui practitioners believe that the ideal situation is for land to slope gently from the east to the west so that a property is higher on the east side than on the west. Terraces that face west or sunken gardens on the west side of the garden are considered very auspicious.

The west is believed to correspond to the disruptive energy of the Celestial Tiger, which is best kept subdued and in balance with the rest of the celestial creatures by being placed at a slightly lower level.

If your terrace faces west, do not raise this area visually by planting trees or shrubs that can grow to a great height. Keep the plantings low and harmonious, incorporating rounded shrubs or trees that correspond to a westerly energy, such as Japanese maples. Also add objects and plantings that symbolize the Fire element, such as lighting and triangular shrubs or trees, and avoid using objects and plants that correspond to the Earth element.

A stone or brick wall can be used to create a terraced effect in the garden if the terrace is in the northeast or southwest. Consider making a terrace from wooden railway sleepers, if your terrace will be in the easterly or southerly areas of your garden. Retain the natural slope of the land but incorporate a waterfall if the area is in the northerly section.

BALCONIES

Balconies are excellent ways of highlighting attractive views and inviting the energy of nature into an apartment space. However, as a balcony is often accessed by sliding doors, usually made of large panes of glass, it is particularly important in feng shui terms for the balcony not only to frame or create a pleasant view but also to contain the energy that may otherwise travel straight from the apartment's main entrance and out through the balcony.

In feng shui it is most inauspicious for the back door or the balcony sliding doors to be exactly opposite the front door, because the energy will tend to rush straight through the space without circulating, thus giving no benefits to the space. This can easily be remedied by softening the lines of the balcony. Use screens and plants to create a lush garden on the balcony—this will encourage the energy to flow back into the apartment.

CREATIVITY ASPIRATION

This area corresponds to the element of Metal, and its energy can be enhanced by placing items that are metallic or related to Metal, such as metal wind chimes, lucky coins, or a string of bells, on the west side of the room.

Also include objects related to the Earth element, such as a display of your favorite decorative plates or a collection of brown semiprecious stones, such as ironstone, tiger's eye, or jasper. In the productive cycle of elements, Earth is the natural home of Metal. It is important not to have any Fire features in this area, such as a fireplace or candles.

Energies that affect creativity and children in your life come from the westerly direction. Although the energy from this direction can be unsettled, once it is stabilized it can be effectively harnessed to help you either further your creativity or harmonize the energy of your children.

It is important not to disturb or activate this westerly energy. Place only quiet, still objects, such as a statue or some heavy, rounded rocks, in the part of the garden that faces west. The statue should be made of an earthy substance—earthenware or terra cotta—but it can also be made of metal, such as steel or bronze.

As the west resonates with the element of Metal, an attractive feature would be a stone sculpture, something that is full of rounded lines and that represents a peaceful subject, such as a person in contemplation.

FENG SHUI TIP
Stimulating your creativity

If you wish to stimulate one of the eight aspirations for yourself only, you may place an object in the area to which the aspiration corresponds. This object should be made from an element that relates to your dominant personality element. Go back to the chart on pages 12–13 to identify which element dominates your personality.

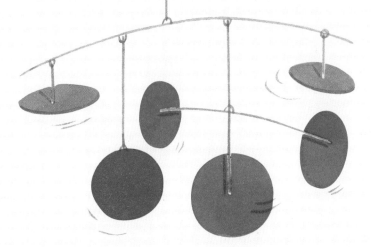

As usual, check this area for poison arrows (see pages 26–27) and clear any clutter in the house or overgrown plants and dead trees or shrubs in the garden. You could even place the sculpture so that it deflects the poison arrows.

An attractive feature in this part of the garden would be a rock garden full of plants that resonate with Earth, such as fragrant herbs and groundcover plants, and plants that have orange and yellow flowers. At the top of the rock garden, place a statue and plant a weeping tree so that its leaves sweep over the top of the statue.

To find your creativity area, see pages 18–21.

CRYSTALS

A FENG SHUI CURE

Crystals are an excellent tool for clearing negative energy from your space. Synthetic crystals, called lead crystal, are faceted crystals made with a certain percentage of lead. Feng shui practitioners also use semiprecious stones as cures.

Faceted lead crystals are particularly useful for breaking up negative energy—hang these over clutter to help disperse the energy built up there.

They will help to clear the clutter and keep the area clear of unnecessary things. If your property has a large formal interior, consider using lead crystal chandeliers as lighting, particularly if the faceting on each piece is even in number. If you have an unpleasant aspect outside your window, such as a blank wall or an industrial plant, hang the crystal in the window to scatter the negative energy and enliven the energy of the room.

Naturally occurring crystals, such as clear quartz crystal, can be placed in the fame and acknowledgment area of your space to stimulate the flow of energy and to enhance your prospects of being noticed (in terms of your career) or being heard (in your family).

Place naturally occurring crystals, such as fluorite, in the corner of your study to ensure that you are able to focus on your work, and to attract success for your exams and assignments. Use a piece of jade in your relationships area to bring stability to your love life. Citrine is an excellent crystal to attract abundance, and can be used in the wealth area of your home or office.

CURTAINS

A FENG SHUI CURE

Curtains and other window coverings are very important in feng shui, as it is considered most inauspicious to leave a window exposed so that when night falls the windowpanes grow dark.

It is thought that darkness encourages the presence of an undesirable and unbalancing amount of yin or passive energy in the home, which will need to be counterbalanced by other remedies, such as leaving lights on and using yang or bright colors in the area surrounding the window.

Flowing lengths of curtains are considered an auspicious method of covering a window, as they mask the corners of the window, which can create poison arrows that also need to be countered.

Curtains are also useful in screening poison arrows created by outside objects—such as electrical supply poles and straight roads that lead to the house—and in covering an undesirable view from the window, which may generate negative energy.

Consider using curtains on your windows if you live near a particularly yang type of place, such as a school, an electrical supply station, an industrial area, a railroad, or an airport, using the fabric to screen you from the strong, aggressive energy created by the movement of a lot of people.

Similarly, use curtains if you live near a particularly yin type of place where there is a buildup of stagnant energy, such as a garbage dump, sewage outlet, a church, or a place of mourning.

FENG SHUI TIP

If you are unsure about incorporating a particular color into a certain room, get a swatch of the color and leave it in the room for a few days. See if the color makes any difference to the energy of the room. For strong imbalances, you may wish to change the color of the walls, but often all that is needed is a couple of cushions or candles in the right color to help balance the energy of the room.

D

DESKS AND OTHER WORKTABLES

If you work at a desk or other tabletop, apply some feng shui principles to your desk to improve your prospects at work. Generally, it is favorable to sit facing the south or southeast direction to attract wealth and acknowledgment qi. However, you could also make your desk face your lucky direction (see "Lucky Directions and Areas" on pages 122–123). Try to make sure that you also sit facing the doorway or opening to your work space. However, you are often unable to move your office furniture to allow for feng shui. If this is the case and your back faces the entrance to your work space, you can cure this bad qi energy by placing a mirror on your tabletop so that the entrance is reflected in it.

There are some golden rules about desks that you should observe:

- Keep your desk and work space neat for the good flow of qi and for safety.
- Keep the drawers of your desk well organized.
- Use a desk that is auspicious in its measurements (see pages 52–53).

If you sit at a desk or use a countertop to make transactions with customers, you may enhance any of the eight aspirations (see pages

ASPIRATION	POSITION ON DESK
Wealth	Top third, left-hand side
Acknowledgment	Top third, middle
Relationships	Top third, right-hand side
Health	Middle third, left-hand side
Creativity	Middle third, right-hand side
Knowledge (getting a promotion)	Bottom third, left-hand side
Career	Bottom third, middle
Travel and mentors	Bottom third, right-hand side

14–15) by mentally dividing the tabletop into the eight sections opposite and placing good luck symbols in strategic places. To encourage good fortune in these areas, place office equipment or good-luck symbols from the table below in the appropriate area.

Recognition, promotions, and profit for yourself and the business can be encouraged by the state of your tabletop. Above all else, your desk must be absolutely clear of clutter. Remove all objects that are not in everyday use and keep your desk drawers neat and functional. Look at your desk and see if there are any areas that are cluttered or corners that have been gathering dust. Keep your desk free of dust, as this symbolizes the fact that you are keeping your work life free of stagnation.

Sometimes clutter arises because you do not have enough space. Consider extending your desk or workplace. However, be ruthless about what you actually need to keep—the more space you make, the more encouragement you give for beneficial qi to circulate through your work life. It is important not to push the clutter out of sight into cupboards or drawers, as this will just continue the stagnation of beneficial qi.

A good way to improve your work life is to have your office or work area decorated harmoniously and ensure that you are not

facing blank walls. If you work at a computer, it is a good idea to take a break near a fountain or other water feature inside or outside the building, as this helps you to avoid building up tension.

OFFICE EQUIPMENT	GOOD LUCK SYMBOL
Cash register, calculator	Three coins tied together with red string
Certificates or diplomas, awards	Luo-pan compass (see pages 20–21)
Family or staff photo, telephone	African violets (*Saintpaulia*)
Lamp	Small piece of jade
Notebook	Small piece of opal
Reference books	The bagua with yin and yang symbol in the middle (see page 17)
Computer	Black tassel
Telephone	Bagua with a convex mirror in the middle

DINING ROOM

The dining room is a place where food and friendship are honored. It is believed that certain feng shui principles must be observed in order to aid digestion. The first aspect to consider is the dining table. The shape of the dining table can enhance a party or destroy it. Circular, oval, or octagonal shapes are best.

Some feng shui practitioners believe that square dining tables provoke arguments because the sharp edges of the table send poison-arrow energy around the table. If you have experienced an increase in arguments around your square table, place a circular or octagonal centerpiece on it.

The table must be able to accommodate an even number of people and it is auspicious to invite an even number of guests. The chairs must be comfortable; if possible, offer your guests chairs with arms instead of side chairs. Chairs with arms, such as carvers, are symbols of the nurturing shape of the landscape that ideally surrounds your house (see pages 23) and symbolize your nurturing attitude toward your guests.

If your dining room is part of the living room, try to screen off the dining area with potted plants or a wooden screen so that there are not too many distractions for your guests. It is believed that distractions cause indigestion.

If family dinners have been less than harmonious, or dinner parties have not gone well, check whether the dining area is affected

---

FENG SHUI TIP

To enhance abundance in your household, place a mirror in the dining room so that it reflects the food. This symbolizes the doubling of your prosperity. Many antique sideboards (especially those made in the nineteenth century) have mirrors in the backboards that gave the impression of extra food and utensils and are also used to double up as backsplashes for meat carving. If you do have mirrors on your sideboard, make sure that you always keep them clean and free from dust and grime. Also check that the silver backing is not wearing off.

by a protruding interior wall, or whether a sharp angle from a pole or a neighboring house can be seen from the table.

If the table has been the scene of disharmony, perform the following ritual to cleanse the area of negative energy:

Step 1 Clear all debris from the table; wash all plates thoroughly and stack away neatly.

Step 2 Remove the tablecloth or place mats; hang outside for a couple of hours.

Step 3 Fill a metal bowl with tap water and add a small cup of hot water in which 2–3 tablespoons of salt (preferably sea salt) have been dissolved.

Step 4 In a circular motion, clean the table with the salty water. Don't worry about scratching the surface of your table—salt crystals that have not dissolved usually sink to the bottom of the bowl. As salt has a yang quality, it is very effective for restarting the flow of energy around the table.

To stimulate harmony at an important dinner party, especially if it is a business dinner, try to incorporate a circular table decoration that includes gold images, such as a golden pineapple. In the West, when the pineapple was first introduced to dinner tables in the eighteenth century, it was regarded as the ultimate symbol of hospitality because of its costliness. In feng shui principles, the pineapple is a golden fruit that is symbolic of abundance and wealth.

For dinner gatherings, make sure that no one seated at the table has his or her back to the door leading into the room; anyone in this position may feel vulnerable or tense. Place a screen between the door and people seated at the dinner table whose backs are toward the door.

DOORS

The front door is one of the most important areas of your home
in feng shui terms because it is the main entrance point for qi.
It is important that your front door is facing the most auspicious
direction for you (see "Lucky Directions and Areas" on pages
122–123) and that it is the recipient of a gentle flow of positive
qi. This can be created by making a garden path that curves to
your door.

It is particularly important that your front door is not
obstructed or not receiving sha qi, or negative energy. Otherwise
known as the "killing breath" or "poison arrows," sha qi can be
created in a number of different ways. The flow of sha qi can be
produced by sharp angles being aimed at your house, for example,
by the sharp angle of a neighbor's roofline or the positioning of a
tower or a pole directly opposite the center of your front door.

You can deflect this negative energy by placing a bagua mirror or
an ordinary mirror above your door. A bagua mirror is an octagonal
disk with a small convex mirror in the center surrounded by the
eight auspicious trigrams (see pages 16–17).

Sha qi also travels along straight lines—a road or an avenue of
trees can lead sha qi to your front door. You can plant a hedge to
deflect it.

Make sure that your front door is in proportion to your house,
and the size of an average person. An entrance that is too large
could lead to loss of money, while a front door that is too small
may constrict the flow of beneficial energy into the house, leaving
the occupants feeling impoverished.

In feng shui, a door or piece of furniture is measured with a feng
shui ruler. This ruler is divided into approximately half-inch

Inauspicious:
Too large a door may
mean a loss of beneficial
energy.

Inauspicious:
Too small a door may
mean a constriction of
beneficial energy.

Auspicious:
Door proportional to
the house.

segments. The divisions all have meanings and are grouped in fours, measuring approximately two inches. The full cycle is approximately sixteen inches. See page 93 for the table of auspicious and inauspicious segments of the feng shui ruler and the associated meanings of each segment. Measure your windows, door frames, furniture, or the room itself to work out whether the dimensions of the objects are causing you bad luck. When larger pieces are measured, the cycle of sixteen inches repeats itself (see page 87).

It is also important that the doors in your house (particularly the front door) do not stick or creak, as this is an indication that energy is not flowing properly through the house. In the workplace, make sure that the doors leading into the office are all in good working order. The doors are symbolic of strong communication of qi between managers and other members of the staff. If the doors stick or are otherwise in disrepair, tension will mount within the department.

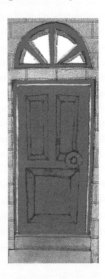

If a young family member's bedroom door gets banged in anger, you can use a special "feng shui ring bell charm" on his or her door to encourage cooperation. The charm is a small bell hanging within a ring. The ring is covered with a knotted cord that ends in a tassel, and the charm can be hung on the inside of the door to your child's bedroom or the front door by a decorative looped cord that is attached to the ring. The banging of doors may also symbolize the attempts of your children to attract more energy so that it will flow to them.

■ FOR **DRIVEWAYS**, SEE **PATHS, PAVEMENTS, AND DRIVEWAYS** ON PAGES 138-139.

EDUCATION: IS IT THE RIGHT COURSE?

SEE ALSO **KNOWLEDGE ASPIRATION** ON PAGES 118–119.

Finding out whether or not you are on the right course in your education or career is a matter of being able to think clearly and determine what you really want from life. Many principles of feng shui are specifically designed so that once a feng shui cure is implemented, your mind is no longer buffeted by negative energies and it will feel clear enough to sort out issues of career path and appropriate studies (see "Concentration" on pages 60–61). However, in the Chinese philosophies underlying feng shui principles, it is believed that the elements (see pages 12–13) play a very important part in our ability to understand ourselves. Our year of birth determines our predominant element. This characteristic governs, among other things, our body type, our personalities, and our preferred modes of work.

In the table below you will see that the last digit of your year of birth indicates which element you resonate with, as well as whether you are a yang (assertive) or a yin (passive) aspect of that element. What type of work is attractive to you is also noted.

Remember that the Chinese New Year starts at various dates, all

DIGIT	ELEMENT	YIN/YANG	PERSONAL WORK BRIEF
1	Metal	Yin	Prefer to have everything in order
2	Water	Yang	Prefer to be an independent consultant
3	Water	Yin	Prefer to work quietly and alone
4	Wood	Yang	Prefer to work in a competitive environment
5	Wood	Yin	Prefer to have a busy workload
6	Fire	Yang	Prefer to work within a team
7	Fire	Yin	Prefer to work with their intuition
8	Earth	Yang	Prefer to work long-term with an employer
9	Earth	Yin	Prefer to work in harmony with coworkers
0	Metal	Yang	Prefer to organize and be in charge

of them later than the New Year in the West. The starting dates for the Chinese New Year vary from about January 21 to February 20. You can use a symbol representing good luck for your element, such as a metal figurine of a rabbit if you were born in a year of the rabbit. You could place this symbol in your home, bedroom, workplace, or desk, in a position that corresponds to a particular aspiration (see pages 14–15) you wish to stimulate. This is the most personalized feng shui cure of all. You could also carry it with you to attract good luck and fortune.

ELECTRICAL EQUIPMENT

Music from stereo systems, televisions, and radios can provide an effective yang energy to counterbalance a dark, yin room. Music that can be heard through the house can stimulate stagnant qi. However, it is important that the sound is not overly loud or discordant.

Generally, you should only have electrical appliances that are necessary in your house. It is thought advisable that the yang energy generated by electrical appliances should be masked when not in use. Television and stereo cabinets, as well as home office cabinets that can house computer equipment, should be considered. If you cannot get this type of furniture, you can use a dark cloth to cover the appliance and neutralize the potentially harmful yang energy. Electrical appliances should not be used in the bedroom because of their potential to disrupt sleep patterns.

Consider using your stereo system and other sound equipment for stimulating the knowledge aspiration area of your house or place of business. See also "Sound: A Feng Shui Cure" on page 159.

Feng shui practitioners also focus on the electromagnetic fields created by electrical appliances used in the home. They suggest limiting exposure to television, computers, and even clock radios (see page 40). Sometimes appliances such as stereo systems can be used in certain areas to stimulate the flow of qi. It is a good idea also to place appliances in a cupboard or storage area when not in use, to reduce clutter.

ELEMENTS IN THE GARDEN

In keeping with the theory of the interconnectedness of everything, the five Chinese elements—Earth, Metal, Wood, Fire, and Water— correspond with certain numbers, compass directions, life aspirations, life paths, seasons, and other aspects of life. Certain common objects can symbolize or represent the elements, such as earthenware pots for Earth, metal gardening tools for Metal, wooden garden furniture for Wood, the barbecue for Fire, and a pond for Water.

In Chinese medicine, the human body is believed to be made of a combination or balance of the elements, so ill health can be rectified by removing certain foods or by adding medicine that resonates with a particular element or combination of elements. Similarly, in feng shui, the elements can be used to rectify an imbalance in the flow of energy around a garden or home.

These five elements are believed to interact with each other in both productive and destructive ways.

Objects and combinations of plantings that reflect the destructive cycle of the elements will attract negative energy in the form of accidents, feelings of unrest, and poor growth. For instance, do not have a pond or water feature right next to the barbecue, as Water is a destructive element to Fire. Remove either one of these features or install an object that corresponds to Wood, such as a wooden deck, so that the destructive relationship between the pond and barbecue is broken.

Harmonious combinations of the elements in garden ornaments and plantings include red roses planted next to a wooden fence

---

FENG SHUI TIP

Place an earthenware pot, lay a paved path, or use any other Earth object or plant (a bed of white flowers, or a weeping fruit tree) near a Fire or Metal area, such as the barbecue area with a metal shed nearby.

(Wood and Fire), a paved barbecue area (Fire and Earth), terra-cotta pots beside a metal gate (Earth and Metal), a metal birdbath filled with water (Metal and Water), and a dense planting of box hedging around a pond (Wood and Water).

EARTH

The element of Earth corresponds with an area that is central in a garden or home, or with the compass directions of southwest and northwest. Garden objects that are symbolic of the Earth element include rock gardens, large terra-cotta pots, brick or stone walls, and clay paving stones forming a path through the garden. Sheds with flat roofs or regular shapes are also symbolic of the Earth element.

Plants that correspond to the energy of the Earth element include herbs that are sweet-smelling and fragrant, such as rosemary and sage, and flowers that are yellow or orange, such as deep yellow chrysanthemums, marigolds, wallflowers, nasturtiums, and primroses. In feng shui, chrysanthemums are believed to evoke a happy and joyful energy in the garden.

In your rock garden, include plants such as yellow rock rose and evening primrose. You can also include roses, such as the miniature 'Ko's Yellow,' in terra-cotta pots. Yew can also be planted, as well as other trees or shrubs that are shaped like a square.

Objects and plants corresponding with the element of Earth must not be placed near objects and plants corresponding with Water, but will benefit the element of Metal. Also, keep Earth

---

FENG SHUI TIP

If you have Wood and Earth arranged together, add a Fire object or a plant nearby to harmonize the energy. For example, plant red flowers in a terra-cotta pot that sits on a deck.

away from the element of Wood, as Wood has a hindering effect on Earth, although the energy of the earth is obviously necessary for the growth of wood.

METAL

The element of Metal corresponds to the energy of fall in the Chinese system of seasons. This is the time when yin energy is beginning to dominate, as the energy of the earth begins to burrow into the ground. This element also corresponds to a westerly direction.

Garden objects that are symbolic of the Metal element include bronze and other metal sculptures, large metal containers, metal dome-shaped structures or spheres, sundials, metal furniture, posts and frames, and tin panels and roofs.

Plants that correspond to the energy of the Metal element include herbs such as yarrow and wormwood. Catnip is also a Metal-element herb—plant it along paths to soften both the color  of the garden and the edges of the path. White flowers such as chrysanthemums, honesty, roses, gardenias, arum lilies, and snowdrops also symbolize Metal.

Plants with gray-green leaves, such as lamb's ears and artemisia, plants with variegated leaves, such as *Coprosma* 'Variegata,' and trees or shrubs that have a circular shape are also characteristic of the Metal element. Objects and plants that correspond to the element of Metal must not be placed near objects and plants that correspond to Wood, but they will benefit the element of Water.

WATER

The element of Water corresponds to the energy of winter in the Chinese system of seasons. This is the time when yin energy is at its strongest, as most of the earth's energy is deeply underground. This element also corresponds to a northerly compass direction.

Garden objects that are symbolic of the Water element include water features such as ponds, fountains, and waterfalls and swimming pools and hot tubs.

Plants that correspond to the energy of Water include plants that are blue or even tending toward black, such as some violets. Other Water flowers include cyclamen, heartsease, and violas. Herbs such as mint, thyme, and chives are considered Water plants.

Trees that are symbolic of the element of Water include silver birch, magnolia, dogwood, juniper, honeysuckle, and tea tree.

When installing a pond, always make sure to keep a water

pump operational at all times and in good condition so that the pond will not become stagnant or overgrown. Around the edges of the pool, plant white flowers or gray-green plants in an undulating line (a "shape" or silhouette that corresponds to the Water element).

Objects and plants that correspond to the element of Water will benefit Wood, and Metal will benefit Water objects and plants. Keep Water away from the element of Earth, as it has a hindering effect on Water.

WOOD

The element of Wood corresponds to the energy of spring in the Chinese system of seasons. This is the time when yang energy is becoming dominant. This element also corresponds to an easterly compass direction.

Garden objects that symbolize the Wood element include wooden furniture, wooden structures such as decks, lattice fences, wooden fences, posts and pergolas, and wicker furniture.

Plants that correspond to the energy of the Wood element include evergreens such as conifers and English box. These trees are dense and green, and are excellent for the edging of a garden or for

---

FENG SHUI TIP

Earth and Water objects and plants must be kept away from each other. They can be reharmonized by adding Metal objects and plants near them. A terra-cotta pot filled with water can be a water feature if it has a metal spout or water pump circulating the water.

screening hedges. Camellias, hydrangeas, and pittosporums, as well as other plants considered rectangular in shape (see pages 52–53), are also symbolic of the element of Wood and are excellent plantings for screening in the garden.

Flowers such as hostas, woodruffs, hellebores, and primulas, as well as such herbs as basil and parsley, also symbolize Wood.

Characteristics of Wood plants include deep, lush green leaves and, usually, dense growth. Plants that do not represent Wood include those that have thorns, pointed leaves, or needles, or that are miniature or bonsai in nature. Roses with thorns, pine trees, and cacti, for example, do not represent Wood.

Objects and plants that correspond to the element of Wood will benefit Fire, and Water will benefit Wood objects and plants. Keep Wood away from the element of Metal, which has a hindering effect on Wood.

FIRE

The element of Fire corresponds to the energy of summer in the Chinese system of seasons. This is the time when yang energies are at their height. This element also corresponds to a southerly compass direction.

Garden objects that are symbolic of the Fire element include barbecues and other cooking apparatus in the garden, such as open ovens, and pointed structures used in supporting trailing plants,

---

FENG SHUI TIP

If you have a destructive arrangement of Metal and Wood (such as a metal shed and dense greenery), add a Water feature or plant to reharmonize the energy. For instance, do not combine wooden fence palings with metal posts or place a wooden seat under a weeping willow.

---

particularly red tomatoes. Plants that correspond to the energy of the Fire element include those that produce red flowers, fruits, or leaves, and those with sharp leaf shapes or spiky thorns.

Triangle-shaped plants also resonate with the element of Fire. Fire plants include pine trees, firs, cypresses, bird of paradise shrubs, bamboo, and crimson-leafed plum trees. In feng shui, bamboo, like the pine tree, is symbolic of longevity.

Fire flowers include red roses, lupins, dahlias, bromeliads, tulips, daffodils, irises, snapdragons, and gladioli. Herbs that evoke the Fire element energy include chilies, leeks, garlic, dill, and asparagus.

It is important to be sparing with Fire plants, though, as the strength of their energy, through color or through scent, may overwhelm surrounding plants. These plants always look their best when planted against a foil of rich, deep green foliage.

Objects and plants that correspond to the element of Fire must not be placed near objects and plants that correspond to Metal, but will benefit Earth. Wood will benefit Fire objects and plants.

■ FOR **ENTRANCE DOOR**, SEE **DOORS** ON PAGES 72–73.

FENG SHUI TIP

Use a Wood object or plant to harmonize the energy in a Water and Fire area. For instance, install a wooden lattice fence between a water feature and the barbecue area.

F

FAMILY ASPIRATION

To enhance the flow of beneficial qi in the area of your house that
corresponds with a harmonious family, turn to pages 18–21 to
identify your family area. To bring greater harmony to the family,
place a brightly colored fan or a flute decorated with bright green
and yellow ribbons somewhere in the interior, as well as checking
for imbalances between yin and yang energy (see pages 10–11) and
areas of clutter that need tidying. Also, place photographs and
paintings of your family members in this area.

Communication is one of the most important
considerations when dealing with relationship issues in
marriage, friendships, or within your family. Make sure
that the doors leading into the family area are all in
good working order, as they are symbolic of strong
communication of qi between the rooms.

If the doors stick or are otherwise in disrepair,
tension will mount within the house. In feng shui, the front and
back doors must not face each other, nor should three doorways
be aligned along a corridor. Place a screen near the back door,
shielding the door from sight of the front door. If there is a
doorway between the front and back doors, place a beaded or
lace curtain or a wind chime in the doorway.

The family area also corresponds with your health and that of
your family. The bathroom will often be located in this area (see
pages 38–39).

It is important to know the lucky direction of each member of
your family (see pages 122–123). Living in a house that resonates for
only some family members can cause enormous difficulties and
clashes. Also check the elemental orientation between family
members and the solutions for those members who are not
elementally compatible (see pages 56–59).

If a member of your family or workforce is feeling particularly
hostile, there are two important aspects that can be changed that

may help to make that person feel more comfortable. First, check whether the person's entrance into the building should be changed. Ideally, it should be suited to her orientation number (see pages 58–59).

Secondly, ensure that the person is sleeping with her head pointing in her favorable direction and that she is working at her desk or workstation facing her favorable direction. If that direction is not available, choose one of the other three directions that suit her orientation group (see pages 122–123).

A significant rearrangement of the house or office might be needed to make these changes. The benefits, however, can be great.

If you are having continual arguments with a troubled child, remove mirrors from your child's bedroom, or cover them, as it is believed that mirrors reflect a person's image while they are sleeping, making their spirit feel uneasy. Mirrors also reflect light, creating an energy in the bedroom that is too strong. Also check that there are no poison arrows or negative energy flowing where your child habitually sits, works, or (if appropriate) sleeps.

Also consider hanging a bell on the door to encourage more peaceful communication between the two of you—the bell helps to clear stagnant energy from the child's relationship between itself and the outside world. Also consider giving the child a present of a piece of jade (to encourage a sense of stability) or some onyx (for balancing and regulating the emotions).

If an argument has erupted, clear the energy of the space by clapping your hands or ringing a bell in the corners, using sound as a feng shui cure (see page 42 and page 159).

FAMILY OR LIVING ROOM

SEE ALSO **FURNITURE** ON PAGES 92-93.

The auspicious placement of furniture in your living room is one of the key requirements for the beneficial flow of energy. It is important that the backs of chairs and sofas are not facing the front door and that the sofa is placed, if convenient, with its back against a wall.

There is a spot in a room called "the honored guest." This is the chair in the living room or at a dining table that you first see as you enter the room. Try to have this chair facing the doorway and make sure the view (either internally or externally) from this chair is particularly pleasant.

For the rest of the chairs and sofas in the living room, it is auspicious for the seating to be grouped in a circle or in an octagonal formation. This will create friendly conversation. Upholster chairs and stools with soft, comfortable fabric in fluid, harmonious designs. Seat cushions can be tied on to soften the lines of an unupholstered chair. Throw pillows will also help to stimulate the energy of seating furniture (see page 89).

The living or family room usually contains the most expensive pieces of furniture—those bought as display pieces or for entertaining guests. When purchasing expensive furniture, take into consideration the proportions and measurements of the pieces, as these are very important in feng shui. For particularly expensive or regularly used pieces of furniture, get a feng shui ruler to figure out whether your sofa, display cabinet, or bookshelf is auspicious in size.

Try not to allow the television or stereo to overpower the living room. Instead, keep electrical equipment hidden in a cabinet or place a dark cloth over it when not in use.

If your living room has a fireplace, keep it clean and free of ash. If the fireplace is positioned facing west, place a screen mesh in front of the hearth in winter or a decorated fire screen in summer, as the energy from the west is thought to be quite disruptive. Corner fireplaces create the best flow of qi in a living room, as the qi is directed past any corners.

If you are using your fireplace on a regular basis, particularly during an unseasonal snap of cold weather, you may be creating too much yang energy, which needs to be counterbalanced by decorating the fireplace with dark colored ornaments or placing dark greenery (preferably artificial) on either side of the fireplace.

Keep any ornaments and greenery near the hearth free from the ash. During winter, when the fireplace is in constant use, hang a mirror over the mantelpiece to encourage the energy to keep flowing around the house rather than going straight up the chimney.

Be sure to guard against poison-arrow energy emanating from protruding corners in *L*-shaped rooms by placing a plant, some wind chimes, or a mirror in front of the corner. Also make sure that the flow of qi is not stagnant in any alcoves. Stagnation can be avoided by the placement of a colorful lamp, for example.

FENG SHUI TIP

When moving into a new house, always purchase new pillows. This signifies a new beginning and symbolizes that you are leaving your old problems behind you.

FANS AND FLUTES

A FENG SHUI CURE

Fans and flutes are useful for dissipating poison-arrow energy that moves quickly through long, straight corridors and for diffusing the negative energy of an exposed beam. Flutes made of bamboo are often used by feng shui practitioners, and are linked with the element of Wood. They can be used to deflect a poison arrow created by wooden elements in the house, such as columns or straight corridors.

Flutes are particularly useful in deflecting the fast, hard-hitting energy caused by overhead beams. The negative energy effects of exposed overhead beams must be minimized—they are believed to cause innumerable problems with health and emotional stability.

It is particularly harmful to use a desk or sleep in a bed that is situated under a beam. It is believed that sitting under a beam can encourage illnesses ranging from mild headaches to serious diseases. If you sleep under a beam, health problems will occur wherever the beam crosses your body. For example, if you suffer from ulcers, check that you are not sleeping under an overhead beam that crosses your stomach.

Pairs of bamboo flutes can also be used to break the rapid energy flow created by straight lines. They should be placed at a forty-five degree angle to the beam, cornice, or architrave. If they are placed parallel to the flow of energy, they will slow it down only minimally. It is best to position the flutes with their mouthpieces facing downward, and to make sure that they are angled toward each other.

Fans can be used to redistribute fast-flowing energy or to stimulate stagnant energy in the corner of a room. Display the fan opened and use it in your bedroom to keep the romance of your marriage or relationship happy and stable.

Consider using fans and flutes for stimulating the relationship areas of your house or workplace.

FENG SHUI RULER

In feng shui, all furniture and interior features, such as doors and windows, must be in correct proportion to the rest of the room. A feng shui ruler is used to measure these features. The ruler is

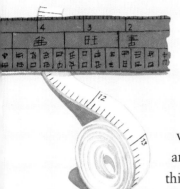

divided into approximately half-inch segments in sixteen-inch cycles, and each segment corresponds to a particular meaning and is categorized as either auspicious or inauspicious.

An auspicious set of dimensions for a work desk or table is between fifty-eight and fifty-nine inches wide, thirty-one to thirty-four inches deep, and twenty-eight to thirty-two inches high. The measurement of fifty-eight to fifty-nine inches attracts success from your creative projects, and thirty-one to thirty-four inches attracts good luck in tests. Other lucky dimensions for larger pieces of furniture include:

- forty-one to forty-two inches—added income from unexpected sources
- fifty-one to fifty-three inches—abundant good fortune
- fifty-nine to sixty-one inches—prosperity and recognition

You can make your own feng shui ruler. Get a long piece of tape, at least ten feet, and mark off every sixteen inches. Then divide each of these sections into eight segments, each measuring two inches. Each of these segments is identified as auspicious or inauspicious:

- The first segment is auspicious.
- The second segment is inauspicious.
- The third segment is inauspicious.
- The fourth segment is auspicious.
- The fifth segment is auspicious.
- The sixth segment is inauspicious.
- The seventh segment is inauspicious.
- The eighth segment is auspicious.

See page 93 for the table of auspicious and inauspicious segments of the feng shui ruler and the associated meanings of each segment.

FISH TANKS

A FENG SHUI CURE

An aquarium of brightly colored fish, such as goldfish, can also be used to balance the yin energy of a room and enhance the flow of wealth into the house. Fish are a very popular feng shui cure, particularly for the wealth aspiration. In Chinese, the word for  "fish" also means "surplus," so having fish in your home or workplace will symbolically encourage the accumulation of wealth beyond your immediate needs, helping you to feel financially secure.

Watching fish swimming in a fish tank is relaxing, and depending on the fish you have chosen and the shape of the tank, may attract abundance and wealth into your home or business.

The best position for the fish tank is in the southeast, the area corresponding to the wealth aspect of your space. Always include some greenery in your fish tank, choosing only those plants that will help your fish to thrive.

Choose red goldfish for your fish tank. The number of fish also affects the flow of energy. You should have six, eight, or nine goldfish in your tank. Do not have four goldfish, although four is a number usually associated with the southeast and the wealth aspiration. In China, four is the number closely associated with death—the way of pronouncing the two words is very similar.

Another belief, one of the few exceptions to the even number rule, is that you should have nine fish in your fish tank—eight goldfish and one black fish. The number eight is auspicious for good business and wealth, while the black fish has the role of "eating" all the negative energy around you.

Remember to keep the fish tank clean and ensure that your fish are healthy and well looked after. Do not allow any clutter around the fish tank and keep the equipment and food necessary for your fish well organized and easy to access.

FLOOR RUGS AND THROW PILLOWS

FENG SHUI CURES

FLOOR RUGS

Floor rugs are useful and relatively easy ways of introducing color into an interior to balance yin and yang energy. For example, a large space with the furniture positioned around the wall could be balanced by a rug, in mainly yang colors such as reds, oranges, and yellows. If the rug is placed in the center of the room, it is best to have some earthy colors in its design, because the middle of the room, as well as the middle of the house, corresponds to the element of Earth.

For most residential interiors, it would be auspicious to choose rugs that have a harmonious blend of colors—a solid block of strong color may unbalance the flow of yin and yang energies within the house.

Auspicious rug designs can include lines of black, which not only give the design strength and definition but also symbolize success and confidence. The designs should be fluid and rounded, rather than angular and geometric. Circular or oval rugs will help to stimulate the flow of energy in a room.

THROW PILLOWS

Throw pillows are a cheap and effective way of introducing differently colored fabrics to a room to balance the flow of energy in terms of yin and yang (see pages 10–11) and the elements (see pages 12–13). Colors such as gold, red, and black are particularly good feng shui colors to introduce into an interior, as they symbolize wealth, good fortune, success, and strength. The softness of throw pillows is also important. This softness represents yin (female) energy, and is an excellent way to balance hard surfaces, such as sofas, chairs, and long low coffee tables, which are symbolic of yang (male) energy.

Always remember to have an even number of throw pillows and make sure they are attractively displayed so that they do not give an impression of clutter.

FRIENDSHIPS

To attract new friends into your life, concentrate on clearing all the clutter in the area of your house, workplace, room, or desk that corresponds to the mentor aspiration. In particular, focus on the northwestern area of your home or office.

If you wish to attract new friends to your family in general, concentrate on clearing the corresponding area of your home. If this space lies in a private space, for example, one of the children's bedrooms, consider placing a lucky feng shui object, such as an image or statue of an elephant, in one of the public rooms, such as the family room, to attract friends and helpful people to you and your family. To find the corresponding area, see pages 18–21.

Follow the practice of checking the chosen area for any poison arrows directed to the room from poles outside or from the corners of internal walls, and implement cures to block any fast-flowing shafts of energy. Ring a melodious bell in the area until you sense a difference. If you do not have a bell, try clapping in the corners where stagnant energy can build up, and also clap over upholstered chairs, sofas, and cushions.

Once the space feels clear, hang a wind chime in a corner of it to increase the possibility of making new friends. This area resonates best with feng shui cures that use melodious sounds. It is an excellent place for your stereo system. However, when you are playing music on your stereo, make sure the sound is not too loud.

Loud sounds overstimulate energy, changing it from a balanced to an aggressive energy.

Introduce more light into this area by hanging a faceted crystal in one of the windows, or by keeping a lamp switched on during the day or night (use a lower wattage bulb to conserve energy). Include mirrors, as well, to reflect the light already coming into the area. Align a mirror on a wall so that it reflects a pleasant arrangement within the room or a view outside your window.

If you feel unworthy of attracting new, compatible friends, place one of the following stones, minerals, or pieces of ore in the mentor/friendship area of your bedroom to encourage friendships:

- Barite (promotes self-assurance and enhances friendships)
- Manganese (strengthens bonds and feelings of cooperation)
- Pyrite (heals feelings of hurt suffered in past friendships)
- Golden topaz (attracts friendships)

If you are seeking useful friends in an office or school environment, such as people in authority who can help you with your career or studies, focus on the area of your desk that corresponds to the mentors aspiration—the right-hand side of your desk at your right elbow. Place your phone in this area to encourage calls from people who are motivated to help you.

The sound of the phone ringing will also stimulate the flow of beneficial energy toward strong friendships, becoming a useful feng shui cure in itself. However, make sure that the ring of the phone is, if not melodious, at least not strident.

You should remove the phone from this area if you are constantly getting calls. Constant use may cause an overstimulation of energy—this should be avoided. Instead, consider using your cell phone as a feng shui cure, keeping it on the right-hand side of the desk, either on top of the desk or in an uncluttered, top right-hand drawer. If possible, program your cell phone to have a simple, pleasant melody as its ringing tone.

To encourage compassion and kindness in your friends, place a picture or statue of the powerful Chinese goddess Kuan Yin on a high shelf overlooking the room, preferably where the floor light can highlight the image. Kuan Yin, who is becoming very popular, is the goddess of compassion, and is often depicted holding a lotus flower.

■ FOR **FRONT DOOR**, SEE **DOORS** ON PAGES 72-73.

FURNITURE

Western furniture is usually an assembly of squares and rectangles rather than fluid, rounded shapes and carvings, which would better suit many feng shui principles. However, there are many ways we can incorporate feng shui concepts and minimize some of the poison arrows caused by the edges of furniture.

Also take into consideration the proportions of the furniture and be careful that items are not too big for the room, creating yang energy that will need to be balanced with a yin-colored rug nearby.

Square and rectangular tables are notorious for creating poison arrows of energy. Feng shui practitioners would recommend choosing a circular or oval table with space for an even number of chairs. However, do not despair if you have a square or rectangular table—consider some of the following suggestions:

- Keep a tablecloth, preferably printed with a fluid pattern, on the table at all times.
- Use round or oval place mats at meal times to minimize the outbreak of arguments and disagreements (these can be aggravated by sharply angled pieces of furniture).

FENG SHUI TIP

Outdoor dining will also be more harmonious if you make sure that the table is oval or circular and that there is an even number of chairs. It is important that no chair back faces the main entrance into the outdoor dining space. Seat your guests in the "honored guest" position—facing the entrance to the dining space. If you are dining under a pergola, make sure that the rafters or roof battens are covered for the evening with, for example, a pretty piece of all-weather cloth.

- On the table, place a circular glass bowl, filled with water, perhaps a couple of floating candles (always an even number), and some flowers or pretty leaves. Make sure the bowl is in proportion to the table.

The shelves of open bookcases also cause poison arrows, so it's worth reconsidering the need for bookshelves in your home or office. If you do need them, never have them positioned so that the poison arrows they create are aimed at your back or your head. If you sit with your back to a bookcase, you may find that you suffer from back pain or from backstabbing colleagues. If you sit facing a bookshelf or have a hutch over your desk or study area, you may suffer from headaches and eyestrain. Another solution is to add glass doors to an open bookcase—this will help to screen the flow of poison arrows.

FENG SHUI TIP

This table indicates the associated meaning of the various segments of a feng shui ruler:

MEASUREMENT	AUSPICIOUS OR INAUSPICIOUS?	MEANING
0-2 in.	Auspicious	Money and abundance
2-4 in.	Inauspicious	Bad luck, legal difficulties, and death in the family
4-6 in.	Inauspicious	Bad luck, theft, and loss of money
6-8 in.	Auspicious	Successful children and helpful people
8-10 in.	Auspicious	Honor and reward
10-12 in.	Inauspicious	Loss and disgrace
12-14 in.	Inauspicious	Disease and scandal
14-16 in.	Auspicious	Abundance

G

GARDEN ENTRANCE

The entrance to your garden and the path leading to the front door of your home should be one of your first concerns when focusing on making your garden a new haven for the beneficial flow of positive energy. Stand at the entrance to your garden and assess how the energy is reaching it.

Energy usually flows to a property along the road, generally in the direction of the traffic on your side of the street. This energy flows beneficially if the street curves, reflecting the gentle flow of a river or stream. On streets that are straight, the qi moves too fast; planting trees and shrubs along the street can slow down this energy. As front boundary lines and our fences are generally in a straight line, it is important to plant along the outside of the fence, particularly if it is a solid stone, wood, or brick wall that does not allow qi to filter through. Set out curved garden beds along your fence line using low-growing fragrant plants and herbs, such as lavender, scented geraniums, and some species of thornless roses, to attract the flow of qi to your front garden entrance.

Next, assess how the energy is flowing through the garden to the front door. Walk through the garden in the way you usually use to get to the front door. Are there any straight lines? You may already have a meandering path to your front door, which is ideal.

If the path is straight, redesign it so that it has a gentle curve (see pages 138–139) or, if you can't replace it immediately, try softening the edges with fragrant plantings, such as lavender, heliotrope,

THE A-Z OF FENG SHUI

hyacinths, or carpet roses, and plant some groundcover plants along the edges so that they will encroach upon the edges of the path. Again choose fragrant groundcover plants such as rosemary, verbena, and thyme.

GARDEN FURNITURE

As the garden is being used more and more as an extension of the house, the placement of outdoor furniture in newly created "garden rooms" needs to follow some of the same feng shui rules that apply to the placement of furniture inside your home.

For instance, when positioning a seat or a swing in the garden or on the porch, make sure that the back of the seat or swing is not facing an opening to that garden area, or a side street, or the entrance to the porch. For children, this will help to reduce the chance of accidents occurring, as they will not feel vulnerable and restless swinging with their backs toward the main flow of energy into the area where the swing is.

Also take into consideration the harmonies between the elements. For example, you can place a wooden garden seat around a tree that is shaped like a triangle, representing the element of Earth, as this element is no threat to Wood. However, do not place a wooden seat around a plant that represents the element of Metal, such as a weeping plant or one that is circular in shape, as Metal is detrimental to Wood.

Wooden furniture is auspiciously placed in the east, southeast, and south; metal furniture is best placed in the north, northwest, or west. However, if the energy from the west is already too disruptive, consider placing metal furniture only in the north or northwest. Also, pieces of metal furniture are best placed by a stone wall or near a water feature.

Pieces of stone furniture resonate with the element of Earth and are best positioned in the center of the garden, in the southwest, or in the northeast. In a formal garden, a centrally placed stone seat anchoring the energy of the garden with the element of Earth would be a harmonious setting. Make sure that the seat has its back protected—with dense green shrubbery, for instance.

GARDEN LIGHTING

Exotic-looking lanterns filled with patterned and colored glass, citronella candles in tall glasses, bamboo flares, and Christmas lights tucked into dense, dark greenery all stimulate the circulation of beneficial energy around the garden.

Garden lighting essentially generates yang energy; it can be used to balance the yin elements in the garden, such as water features, and in dark corners of the garden where the energy may slow down too much and become stagnant. Generally, avoid strong, glaring lights unless you are remedying the flow of disruptive energy that comes from the west or is created by a poison arrow.

Garden lighting can also improve security in your property. Often, security is breached at points where poison arrows hit a fence line, window, or door. For instance, on the back porch keep a light permanently on (use a low-wattage light to minimize cost and energy use) if you can see a pole, roofline, or the corner of a garden structure directly in line with the back door.

Use an upward-pointing light in your front yard if the street is higher than your front entrance, or if the west side of your property is higher than your east side.

In feng shui, it is important to light garden paths and gates. This helps the beneficial energy—not to mention your evening guests!— find its way to your front door or through your garden to your outdoor dining setting without mishap.

Should any accidents occur outdoors in the evening, rectify the poor energy flow in that area by adding some lighting. The extra light will help everyone see where they are going, and will also add yang energy to stimulate the flow of qi in the area.

Also add light in the southerly part of your garden, particularly in your front yard, which represents the public side of your life, to attract a promotion or acknowledgment at work.

GARDEN ORNAMENTS

You can easily encourage the flow of beneficial energy around you by using ordinary garden ornaments. Just take care to follow the basic principles of feng shui concerning the balance between yin and yang (see pages 10–11) and the elements (see pages 12–13).

In dark, shady areas of your garden, possibly tucked away from the main garden, include a brightly colored garden ornament to balance the yin energy of the spot and create an aesthetically pleasing tableau, which will help to generate good energy and add to the power of the beneficial energy already circulating around the garden. Also, if the direction is appropriate (such as south), use objects that are spiky or triangular, such as birdhouses, to add the energy of Fire to the space.

Other ordinary garden ornaments that resonate with the element of Fire include pyramid-shaped garden stakes for supporting plants such as tomatoes. However, be careful to avoid sharply angled decorations such as weather vanes or square planters for trees that won't be covered or softened by plants.

Metal garden ornaments, such as stainless steel metal balls and flat metal silhouettes of fairies or other mythical creatures, can be placed in either the northwest or the west. Metal sculptures of frogs or cranes complement the energy of water features, which are often beneficially placed in the north.

As with the use of feng shui cures to balance the flow of energy in a space, do not overuse garden ornaments, as this may lead to the area feeling cluttered and overstimulated.

Also consider placing flags, mobiles, and other feng shui cures that move with the wind in your garden to create interest and to stimulate the movement of beneficial energy.

GARDEN STATUES

Garden statues of dragons in the easterly part of a garden, a phoenix in the south, and a tortoise in the north invoke the energy, respectively, of wisdom, good luck, and nurturing. Statues that represent yang energy, such as dragons, are best placed in shady areas to balance the yin energy of the space, while yin energy statues (for example, those where the image is in a meditative pose) are best placed in sunny, dry areas of the garden.

The tiger of the west is rarely incorporated into the garden, as this creature represents a potentially disruptive energy that really needs to be left alone and undisturbed. However, its image can be used as a symbol of protection if it looks benign rather than aggressive. Use a garden statue that represents calm and wisdom, such as the image of a seated Buddha, in the westerly area.

Incorporating important spiritual figures, such as the Buddha and the popular goddess of compassion (Kuan Yin), in any aspect of the garden is considered auspicious as long as the images are

treated with honor and respect. Place these statues in areas of honor—for instance, on a ledge or pedestal above the ground in a space that is seen as soon as a person enters that section of the garden. Do not place them anywhere near a sewage outlet or the compost heap.

Incorporate an image of a frog in your pond to stimulate further good luck for any of your financial ventures. If you have a large water feature in your garden, such as a swimming pool, consider placing a statue of a dragon turtle between the pool and your house. A dragon turtle has the head of a dragon and the body of a turtle, and is an excellent feng shui cure, counterbalancing the overly yin energy created by the pool. Similarly, if your house faces a huge body of water, such as a water reservoir, place the statue in front of your house so that it is facing the water feature.

GARDEN STRUCTURES

It is important that garden structures do not create poison arrows that cause disruptions in the flow of energy in the garden. Stand by your front door and see if there are any sharp angles created, in particular, by your gate. If you have a pergola or roofed gate over your driveway or entrance, make sure that the structure is not casting any poison arrows in the direction of your front door, or toward any part of your garden.

If the roofline is hitting a particular area, consider adding a decorative or practical feature to the end of the roofline—perhaps a drainpipe leading down to the ground, or a small terra-cotta figurine (one on each side of the roof for balance), or a pair of bells, pagoda-style.

Grow a tall shrub in front of any vertical wood, stone, or brick post that is part of the entrance to your property, and in front of any other sharply angled structures in the garden. If you wish to sit under a pergola that has a number of exposed beams overhead, plant climbers that will grow up to cover them and that will create an auspicious circulation of beneficial energy—try wisteria, clematis, honeysuckle, or scented jasmine.

While you are waiting for these plants to grow, you can counter

the overwhelming downward-bearing energy created by the beams of the pergola by tying red ribbons on each beam and hanging a basket of flowers and plants from each of the major structural beams.

Soften the corners of garden sheds and other small buildings in the garden with plants or by hanging a crystal or wind chime in front of the corners. Do not have your child's playhouse facing west. Ideally, it should face the east, as it is believed that the energy from this direction, which represents the attainment of wisdom and knowledge, is excellent for helping children to learn and develop their skills.

GIFTS

UNCLUTTERING STRATEGIES

Gifts are an important expression of regard and respect for the person receiving them. However, there are situations in which friends and relatives feel overly stressed about buying a gift, and sometimes little care or time is taken to select the most appropriate expression of their feelings for you.

Gift-giving is an art, and it doesn't always work out right—many of us have a cupboard full of objects that we would rather not own. However, we may cherish the thoughts that our friends and relatives have sought to convey.

One way of dealing with this conflict between an unsuitable gift and the genuine expression of love or friendship it represents is to have a special box that will hold your favorite cards, as well as a photograph of the items that various people have given you that have been unsuitable but well meant. This leaves you free to give or throw away the gift without throwing away the love and affection.

To avoid future gift-giving disasters, consider sending short gift lists to whoever asks. When giving a present to a friend or relative,

---

FENG SHUI TIP

Why should you be careful about accumulating clutter? The more objects you accumulate, the more you become bogged down with maintaining the clutter you have. If you calculate the time and money you spend on storing, removing, cleaning, and organizing your treasures, you may be surprised to see how little time you have left for the things you actually want to do. It is not only your time that may be lost. Robbery and theft are serious concerns. Thieves may be attracted by the saleable commodities in your home or office space. Many people use security systems and have people watch their houses while they are away. This can also be costly.

---

do not be afraid to ask for a gift or wish list—coordinate with other friends or relatives to make sure no one doubles up.

Also, when you are with friends or relatives, if they mention they would like a particular item, make a note of it as soon as you can in your journal or notebook. Have a page for each friend and relative that you usually give presents to, and jot the ideas on the person's page.

Get family members to pool their money and purchase one large functional or good-quality gift instead of giving a number of small, unusable items. Establish ground rules with your family and friends about alternative gift ideas—this may help to alleviate the levels of clutter in your home.

There are many thoughtful ways to share your love, regard, or respect for another person. You could make a gift bag for a friend into which, every year, you pop a small expression—a beautiful collection of stones, shells, or feathers, for example—of your regard for that friend. Another noncluttering solution is to take your friend or relative out to a restaurant or cook the person a meal at home. You could give a box of homemade cookies, a bunch of flowers from your garden, or a terra-cotta pot planted with a small "garden" of flowering bulbs. Your resourcefulness and the thought and care you put into simple expressions of your regard will be greatly appreciated.

H

HEALTH ASPIRATION

The eastern section of a building or garden corresponds to the
family/health aspiration. Focus on this area in the home or
workplace if you wish to improve the longevity and health of your
family or staff. To protect the health of your family, clear the eastern
section of your home by counteracting poison arrows (see pages
26–27) and removing the clutter from this area.

Also focus on the master
bedroom, which is the symbol
of the head of the family. It is
particularly important to keep
the master bedroom clear of
clutter and poison arrows,
because this bedroom is
symbolic of the state of the
whole family, including those who grew up in the house but no
longer live at home. As a protection against ill health, clear the
eastern part of the master bedroom—or the middle of the wall on
the left-hand side of that room as you are looking into the room
from the door—and then include an appropriate feng shui cure in
either place.

If you are suffering from an undesired quick turnover of staff in
your business, there may be too much yang or overly strong energy
shooting through the workplace. Place a representation of one of
the creatures listed on the next page in the health area to encourage
a flow of beneficial energy to your staff.

If last-minute rushes, poor timing skills, and a general sense of
apathy exist in your workplace, there may be too much yin or overly
passive energy around, slowing the energy so much that it has
become stagnant. Place a piece of citrine unobtrusively in the
eastern section of the staff room.

If a family member is suffering from ill health, focus on the
bed that person is using. The position of the ill person's bed is

particularly important. Feng shui practitioners believe that an inauspiciously placed bed can have a powerful effect on health. It is important that the bed is placed in the room so that the person lying in it can see the door. Move the bed if:

- It is under a beam or below a toilet.
- The headboard shares a common wall with the toilet.
- It is directly under a window.
- The footboard is pointing directly out the door (this is called the "coffin" or "mortuary" position).

If possible, place a feng shui cure in the window to attract beneficial energy. Cures include a special five-coin charm that ends in a circular piece of white jade with a hole in the middle.

The eastern part of the bedroom also corresponds to health. Place all the medicines that are required for the illness in this area. Also include in this area a picture or jade figurine of a cicada, an ancient symbol of longevity and health.

Three gourds can be placed on the ill person's headboard to counter long-term ill health, and a picture of an elephant, a symbol of strength, can also be included in the bedroom to help clear the energy.

In feng shui there are a number of symbols of longevity that can be incorporated into the home or business—these will stimulate a strong life force that will improve your personal health and increase the odds that your business will survive and flourish. Of course, in feng shui it is important that this energy force is not overwhelmingly strong, as balance is an essential key to the proper beneficial flow of energy.

Images of animals always play an important role in evoking a sense of longevity and endurance. Place pictures or other representations of one of the following creatures in the eastern section of your home to attract long life and good health:

- Bat
- Cicada
- Crane
- Deer
- Horse
- Monkey
- Rabbit
- Tortoise

HOME OFFICE

If you work from home, either occasionally or on a full-time basis, consider implementing a routine cleansing of your home office, preferably after a major project has ended or before planning to attract new clients. Some freelance workers find that they do this automatically, as they have an instinctive urge to "clear the decks" before new work comes in. In both feng shui and nature magic, it is believed that the sheer act of clearing "old energy" encourages "new energy," sometimes in the form of new clients or work, to enter your life.

A cleansing in the home office can entail anything from neatening your files or tools to rearranging the furniture. Make sure your office space is dust free. Wipe your tabletop clean. Neaten your books, files, tools, and equipment, and assess whether you need to store your past files in the office or find off-site storage.

Overwhelming clutter in the office can lead to an inability to carry your work through to a satisfactory conclusion. Keep your workspace as clear as possible of files or books representing past jobs. If you do not, you may find that your energy is caught up with the past.

FENG SHUI PRINCIPLES FOR BALANCE IN YOUR WORK

1 Never have your desk or office space in your bedroom, because this will interfere with your sleep. If your desk is in your bedroom, separate the two areas with a screen, bookshelf, or large plant.

2 Never sit at your desk or workbench with your back facing the door, because you may feel vulnerable and insecure in this position.

3 Move your desk to face your favorable direction (see pages 122–123), because you will then be able to tap into a beneficial energy flow.

4 Do not have shelves in the office unless they are covered by a cabinet door.

5 If you have a choice, position your home office in your wealth, acknowledgment, career, mentor, or knowledge areas.

6 Do not face a blank wall. Position an inspiring picture (not a mountainscape) or words above your desk.

7 Make sure that the view from your home office is tranquil, because an overactive, or yang, view will be overstimulating, causing headaches and an inability to focus.

TIPS FOR THE HOME OFFICE

You can stimulate your business acumen by placing a naturally pointed clear crystal or cluster of clear crystals in each corner of your home office. Hanging a faceted clear quartz crystal over the telephone or the fax machine will stimulate work-related calls. To stimulate new business, place a red tassel in the wealth corner of your home office. In your home office, make sure your furniture is in proportion to the office space.

Working at home has the disadvantage that it is often difficult to confine your job to normal working hours because of deadlines or expectations. Position your home office somewhere separate from your relaxation areas. If your office is not in a separate room, ensure there is a clear division between your work and home space, using screens and potted plants.

If you have open bookcases in your home office, consider placing glass or solid doors on them to shield you from the poison arrows created by the horizontal lines of the shelving. If you sit with your back to an open bookcase, you may feel that people are talking about you behind your back. To counter this, hang a six-coin charm from the back of your chair.

If you are constantly trying to meet deadlines, make sure that your clock is not facing the main entrance or front door. You do not want time to run out on you!

HOUSEHOLD CLUTTER

UNCLUTTERING STRATEGIES

Vital energy comes into your home or business space primarily through the front door or the front entrance from the street. Keep this area well aired and free from clutter. Do not store broken items or parts of larger objects in this area—they will block beneficial qi energy from freely entering your space. Also, do not keep shoes around the front door. If you must leave them there, purchase a box in which to put them.

Clutter generated by your children is another important area for which you should consider devising an appropriate system. Place all their papers and homework in one area, but first ask your children where they would like to put their homework and what type of container they need. If your children are allowed to choose how they want to store their paperwork, there will usually be a higher level of compliance and a lower level of clutter—they have become part of the decision-making process, contributing significantly to the clutter solution. Continue to keep them involved in routine clutter sessions, and in reevaluating your family's organizational systems.

Paper clutter is one of the biggest problems in any family. Where to begin? Start by locating the various bits of paper that make up the clutter. Usually there are piles of paper and magazines in briefcases, on desks, entry tables, kitchen benches and drawers, and in home offices, garages, sheds, and cars.

FENG SHUI TIP

When shopping for household items, do not buy things just because they are on sale. Take the time to research prices, compare features, and shop around for the best deals. When purchasing dinner sets and other dishes, stick to one pattern and a plain color or design that matches the pattern and can be used for everyday ware. Ensure that you will be able to buy replacement pieces, and do not stray from your selection.

Sort these papers into broad categories, such as financial, business, and personal. Then take one pile, say "personal papers," and sort it into subcategories, such as evening courses, local events, and movie listings. Make sure you file only the most current information and review the subcategories regularly.

If you have a home office, make sure that you can have a separate room for your office and that the paper it attracts and generates is kept separate from the household paper clutter. Develop strategies and timetables to ensure a balance between work and home life, and make time for regular uncluttering in both home and office areas.

If you don't have time to read the daily paper, think about whether or not you need to buy it every day. Perhaps purchase a newspaper only on the days when you will have time to read it. Virtually every newspaper has a website that can give thumbnail sketches of the main stories of the day, so you could incorporate a quick Internet newspaper session each day. If you do buy newspapers, make sure that they are discarded as soon as they have been read (cut out any articles you need to keep first)—they are a fire hazard and can be an emotional drain.

When you have finished uncluttering the various areas in your home and office, light a candle in that area and do something celebratory, such as having a house clearing party. If clutter starts to appear again, check for any hidden poison arrows (see pages 26–27) or seek professional feng shui advice.

HOUSEWARMING

Before you buy or rent a home or workplace, feng shui practitioners would advise you to ask about the former residents or occupants. Why are they leaving the premises? Have they had to downsize their business?

It is important to learn whether the previous owners of your house suffered mental illnesses, divorce, or untimely death while living in the house. Be wary if the house is being sold as part of a divorce settlement.

If the premises become available because the occupiers have come into money and bought a bigger home, or because the occupiers' business has expanded and bigger premises are needed, there is a great chance that this space has a good flow of energy. If residents are moving for different reasons, however, reconsider moving in.

If you do continue with the purchase or agreement to rent, there are a number of ways you can cleanse the accumulated negative energy from the space and attract a better flow of energy into your home life or business.

It is important to start by cleansing the area physically. Have all surfaces washed and all carpets cleaned. Consider repainting and even changing the carpet. Look at buying plants and using fabrics made from natural fibers.

Next, check if the environment of the house is too yin or passive. This can occur if the house is dark or next to a yin environment such as a cemetery, church, garbage dump, or sewage outlet. If this is the case, you will need to stimulate the energy flow of the environment. The simplest way to relieve stagnation of energy in your home is to place a bagua, with a concave mirror in the middle of it, over your front door—the main entrance through which beneficial energy enters your home.

Strong yang colors such as red, orange, yellow, or gold can also be used to stimulate energy in dark areas. Use red, black, and gold to stimulate the flow of a prosperous energy in your home.

Then check if there are poison arrows aimed at the house (see pages 26–27). Walk around your home or check the view from the front door and windows of your apartment.

Once you have cleared the energy of the new premises, walk through the house ringing a melodious sounding bell in each room and in each corner (see page 24). Start from the front door and move through your new home in gentle curves, making sure that you ring your bell in every room.

At this point, consider holding a housewarming party (for tips about an office-warming ceremony, see pages 134–135). The term "housewarming" comes from the ancient Roman and Greek traditions of transferring glowing embers from the hearth of a family's old home to the hearth of their new one. This practice stems from the belief that the spirits protecting the house live in the hearth. These household spirits were thought to be in charge of the family's luck and sustenance. If the glowing embers were moved, the spirits could continue protecting the family.

Therefore, to introduce personal, positive energies into your new home or workplace, you should have a housewarming party after you have neutralized your space by cleaning it. Consider asking your friends to bring a personal blessing for you. Get them to write their good wishes on paper. Then, during the party, light your hearth, burn all the papers with sage, and fan the smoke around the house. If you do not have a hearth, use a large metal bowl half filled with sand. Burn the papers in a small pile in the middle with a sprinkling of sage over the top.

I

IDEAL HOME AND LOCATION

If you are in the enviable position of starting afresh and want to use feng shui to choose your new house, consider using the following checklist as it may help you to narrow your choices. The checklist has been devised in the form of questions to which you can respond either "yes" or "no." A house that has inspired no more than three negative responses should be placed on your list of possible homes.

In feng shui, it is considered prudent to avoid living near areas or buildings that have a poor balance of yin and yang energy. Schools traditionally have an excess of yang energy and can cause people living near them to feel a low-level sense of unease.

Students living near their college or university should take care to go away for breaks between semesters to recover fully from being exposed to very strong yang energy. This is less necessary if the buildings of the college or university are not densely packed and are balanced with large expanses of grass and trees. Similarly, living near electrical lines, airports, or areas that attract a lot of human traffic, such as train stations and factories, should be avoided.

Places that are excessively yin in energy are characterized by an association with death, grieving, and feelings of distress. It is best to avoid living near churches, graveyards, and police stations. Sewage plants and garbage dumps create a stagnant energy that causes negative energy to pervade your home. Since the practice of extending shorelines or filling in undesirably shaped terrain with landfill is common, check that your new house, apartment, or townhouse was not built upon reclaimed terrain.

LOCATION

1. Is the street reasonably quiet and free from heavy traffic?

2. Does a road run past the house?

3. Is there a hill or bank of trees at the back of the property?

4. Is the front of the property free from obstruction (pole, factory, or other large building)?

5. Is the property near a lake or park?

6. Is the property situated away from electrical lines?

7. Is the property situated away from a school (outside a one-mile radius)?

8. Is the property situated away from a graveyard (not in view of the house)?

9. Is the property built on land other than a landfill or garbage dump?

10. Is the property situated away from a church or funeral home (outside a one-mile radius)?

11. Have the previous occupants been free from physical or emotional illness and divorce?

12. Is the house free from a history of upheaval or violence?

THE PROPERTY

1. Does the plot of land have a regular shape?

2. Is the house regularly shaped?

3. Is the house situated either in the middle or toward the front of the plot of land, with a good-sized front yard?

4. Is the front door of the right proportions for a person of average size?

5. Are the rooms regular in size?

6. Is the front door situated in a northerly direction?

EAST/WEST ORIENTATION

1. Does the front door face any of your lucky directions?

2. Does the position of the house correspond with your east/west orientation?

3. Does the bedroom allow you to place your bed in your lucky direction?

4. Does the room of your potential home office allow you to place your desk in your lucky direction?

INSECTS

A FENG SHUI CURE

The category of insects includes butterflies and
cicadas. These insects are often incorporated into
Chinese art, as part of the scenes of flowing
landscapes depicted on screens, wall hangings,
and beautifully translucent porcelain bowls and
dishes. Symbols of these creatures can be used in

an interior to invoke a certain type of energy. Many of these insect
symbols can also be found carved in various semiprecious stones,
such as green jade.

The butterfly is a symbol of joy and attracts positive energy into
the house. Place an unframed picture of a butterfly where there is a

lot of space, to encourage a more carefree feeling
to enter your life. It is important not to have the
butterfly image closely surrounded by other
objects, as its energy dissipates quickly if stifled.

The cicada is a symbol of joy, as well as having
the mythic quality of being able to promote

immortality. A cicada carved in jade, a stone that is often used for
symbols related to health, is used by some feng shui practitioners to
counter illness in the house.

FENG SHUI TIP

The aspiration that relates to your health and the flow of
harmony among your family members corresponds to the area
of your garden that faces east. If you are constantly experiencing
health problems, concentrate on improving the garden in this
area. Place an image or a wooden sculpture of a dragon in this
area, and surround it with plants and objects that correspond to
the element of Wood (see page 23), such as a pergola or an
arbor. Make sure that the image is a peaceful one and the dragon
does not appear to be fierce. Dragons are traditionally placed in
the eastern part of the garden. However, they can also be
positioned to counterbalance any powerful negative energy
aimed at your garden or home.

INTUITION AND FENG SHUI CURES

There are many people who instinctively know about the flow of energy in their house or place of business and who follow their intuition unconsciously, understanding how to make the most of their environment. Often, the homes of these types of people are comfortable and a joy to visit.

Many of us, to some degree or other, have a feeling about what would look good in a particular room, although we don't know why. The placement of a potted palm in a certain corner may be satisfying to us, without our realizing that the plant now shields us from a poison arrow created by a protruding corner. It is important to follow your intuition about the way your home feels. Your feelings may also be in tune with the seasonal variations of light and warmth, making you put warm yang colors in a southeast room that is decorated in forest greens. It is sensible to follow such instincts.

At times, though, there may be some areas that just don't work, no matter what you try. This is where feng shui becomes particularly useful, by helping you to identify where the qi is stagnating and choosing the feng shui solution that will encourage the energy to flow harmoniously through the area.

It is also beneficial to use your intuition when deciding how many feng shui cures you are going to use at once. Make the most appropriate changes and allow a period of time to elapse to see if you can sense any subtle changes in the way the affected area feels. Usually it doesn't take long for the energy to realign itself. Make sure you only try a few cures at a time, as too many cures may become clutter.

JOB INTERVIEW

One of the most common problems in a job interview situation is being seated where your back is facing the entrance to the interview room. When you are placed in this position, you are more likely to feel nervous and unable to project yourself in the best possible light. Try to move the chair so that you are facing the doorway and are not so vulnerable. If this is impractical, don't worry, as there is a way to shield yourself unobtrusively from the energy hitting your back.

If you have a good sense of direction, roughly work out which compass direction the windows of the room face so that, when in the interview room, you can try to sit facing one of your lucky directions (see pages 122–123).

Take a black bag or briefcase into the interview room. In feng shui, black symbolizes strength and determination. If you are unable to reposition the chair, simply place the bag behind the chair, as if you are putting it out of the way (after you have removed the files or other documentation you might need during the interview, of course). The bag will act as your shield against negative energy.

Have a gold feng shui coin nestling near your documentation to encourage success in your interview. Some feng shui practitioners believe that, to strengthen determination and success, you should also take a small, gold-colored statue of a goat to your interview.

When you are looking for new employment or a new career path, it is always wise to clear the energy in your home and office so that you can make way for new opportunities and ideas. On the morning of the interview, take some time to clear your briefcase, wallet, or purse completely, symbolizing the clearing of old energies to make way for the new. If you are driving to the interview, also clear your car of clutter.

You may hang three tassels inside your briefcase or from your car's rearview mirror. Choose a black tassel for a feeling of confidence, a yellow tassel to symbolize your wish to advance in your career, and a purple tassel to help you attract the best remuneration possible.

If you want some extra help, hang the tassels in front of the mirror in your car (just for the duration of the interview—remove them once you are ready to drive away) or keep them in a compartment of your briefcase or bag in which you have also placed a small pocket flashlight.

Keep the flashlight on during the interview if you know that the light won't show through the bag's zipper and if you won't need to get any documents from your bag. Otherwise, simply place the flashlight with the tassels as a symbol of lighting the path to your goals, which are represented by the tassels.

Job interviews always seem one-sided, with the potential employer having the upper hand. However, you can use your job interview to deduce a number of important facts about the business you hope to be working for to figure out whether you really want to work there. Do you notice clutter in the offices or interview room? This could mean that the organization has problems with its flow of energy. Does the receptionist appear friendly and welcoming? This may indicate that there is a good flow of energy in the company. Make your own feng shui observations.

Before the job interview, consider placing in the career area of your home or workplace one of the following images to help stimulate success:

- A picture of a coiled dragon; ensure that you do not place this before an entrance or doorway.
- A picture of an eagle, which should be placed before a window or door.

KITCHEN

The kitchen is one of the most important rooms for encouraging both abundance and inspiration into your home. In feng shui, the kitchen is a symbol of your family's prosperity. Be careful that your kitchen cannot be seen from the front door. A kitchen in the center of the house is also inauspicious. There are two powerful elements at work in the kitchen—Fire (symbolized by the stove) and Water (symbolized by the sink and the refrigerator).

The state and position of your stove is strongly linked with the state of your fortune. It is important to keep it as clean as possible, in good working order, and to rotate the use of each stove element or burner in a clockwise direction. This helps to move any stagnant energy concerning your finances and may even lead to a healthier bank balance.

In feng shui, it is important that the stove is well positioned in the kitchen and in the house as a whole. Take note of the following principles:

- The stove should not face the door to the kitchen or the front door.
- It should be in a space diagonally opposite the entrance.
- It should ideally face in a southeasterly direction or in the cook's favorable direction (see pages 122–123).

Make sure there is nothing undermining the Fire element that your stove symbolizes, such as water pipes. The element of Water is particularly harmful to the Fire element, as water can put out a fire.

Do not have your sink right next to your oven or stove. If you do, place a (preferably wooden) divider between the two. Also, try to avoid having your oven opposite your stove.

The sink must also be kept in pristine condition. The drain hole must be kept lightly covered by a sink plug at all times. As water is a symbol of wealth in feng shui, it is important that it does not drain away. As leaking taps and pipes symbolize a waste of finances, make sure that these are kept in good condition and are repaired promptly.

Dirty dishes left in the sink are the worst kind of clutter, symbolizing not just an obstruction to generating prosperity in your life, but also "dirt" in the family home, such as unhappy news or a lowering of status.

Keep detergent and other kitchen cleaning products out of sight, neatly organized in a convenient cupboard. Feng shui practitioners also advise having a pleasant view outside or an inspiring picture to look at.

The kitchen is also the place in the house where clutter most often accumulates. The cause may be the inhabitants' erratic lifestyles, reflected in irregular eating habits or an unwillingness to cook. Clutter in this area represents the slowing down of the flow of abundance to you and your family.

If you never seem to have the time to use your kitchen, or often feel reluctant to use it, check whether the energy flow of the room is affected by poison arrows (see pages 26–27). These may be directed either from the kitchen fittings or through the kitchen window. If you have open shelving in the kitchen, consider adding doors to cover it.

Another feng shui issue to consider is whether you have your back to the entrance to the kitchen while preparing or cooking your food. If you find that you can't get anyone to help you with the dishes, the reason may, at least in part, be the fact that being at the sink means having your back to the door. This may make the person at the sink feel uncomfortable.

As a remedy, place a mirror above the sink. Then you will be able to see the door behind you. Use this feng shui cure above the stove, as well as in other important preparation areas that necessitate your facing away from the kitchen door.

KNOWLEDGE ASPIRATION

The acquisition of knowledge, and success in
your studies, corresponds to the northeasterly
direction. In this area of your home, garden, or
workplace, the nurturing energy of the north

combines with the energy of the east, an energy that resonates with
wisdom and culture. To find your knowledge area, see pages 18–21.

To attract success in your studies and opportunities to study, the
knowledge aspiration needs to be stimulated. First, focus on the
places where you spend the majority of your time, such as the bed
and your desk. Unclutter these areas and check that poison arrows
do not affect these parts of your room (see pages 26–27). Feng shui
cures that work particularly well in this area relate to color and
to the energy generated by the electrical equipment necessary for
your work.

To stimulate the knowledge area, it would be best to include
rich, vibrant colors that tend toward yang energy, such as reds,
oranges, pinks, and yellows. However, do not use these colors
indiscriminately—it is important to keep a sense of balance and
harmony in the building. It is better to have splashes of bright color
enlivening the area. Feelings of fatigue and overwork may occur if
this area is subject to an overly yang energy.

Overstimulating any area by overusing feng shui cures can create
negative energy, which results in more energy flow problems. In this
case, the cures merely become clutter, stagnating the energy flow
through your home. If you notice a number of feng shui cures as
soon as you walk into a room, they are not doing their job of
circulating or blending into the flow of energy.

To enhance the flow of energy in the knowledge aspiration,
place a red mat in the knowledge area of
your home, bedroom, or study, and, on
top of it, position a statue of the great
Chinese philosopher Confucius. If you
cannot get a statue, get a color
picture of him and place it in a
metal frame. This cure can also
be placed at the entrance of your
home when you need extra support
with your studies, such as at exam

time. The image at the entrance will infuse the energy flowing through the house.

Similarly, the image of a pagoda is excellent for stimulating success with your studies—some feng shui practitioners recommend that a pagoda image be placed on your bedside table (preferably on the right-hand or yang side of the bed).

If you are planning to study abroad, consider clearing the northwest section of your house as well—it corresponds to the mentors/travel aspiration. Then apply cures to stimulate the energy in this area, such as sound or wind chimes. If the area feels stagnant and uninviting, ring a bell in each corner to clear any stagnant energy and leave the windows open when it is sunny to reenergize the area.

If you are feeling blocked and always tired when you are studying, check whether the study is too yin in energy. This area may feel stagnant and cluttered, echoing your feelings of being overwhelmed by the amount of study you have to do. The first step is to clear this area of your house, garden, office, or desk.

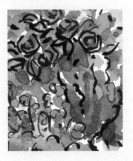

Take some breaks during your studies to work on the corresponding knowledge area in the garden, particularly focusing on improving the soil. Create a space in this part of the garden where you can refresh yourself and tune into the harmonious flow of nature. You could make an attractive feature here by setting up a display of colorful plants and shrubs—particularly those that flower red, orange, and yellow—around an elevated sculpture or lantern that resonates with the shape of a pagoda to attract good luck and success in your exams.

LIGHTS

A FENG SHUI CURE

Lights, mirrors, crystals, and other reflective surfaces are excellent for deflecting poison arrows of negative energy and bringing yang qualities to balance a dark, overly yin room.

Use a low-wattage lightbulb, and leave the outside light permanently on near your front door. This will help to deflect any negative energy projected by an oncoming roadway, power pole, or tower. Alternatively, leave the entrance hall light on permanently. If your front door is below street level, install a light fitting that spreads light upward. This will give the impression that your front door is higher up than it really is.

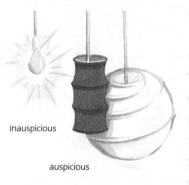

inauspicious

auspicious

Light that floods downward helps energy flow around the house or workplace. Rounded lamp bases are desirable—light will bounce off an angular lamp base and create a movement of negative energy. Use floor lamps that angle light upward to stimulate dark corners, dark-colored rooms, and rooms that do not get much sunlight. These floor lamps will also help to alleviate feelings of depression. Balance is important in feng shui, so make sure you place lamps in pairs where possible.

Consider using lights, mirrors, and crystals for stimulating the acknowledgment and fame aspiration area of your house or place of business (see pages 30–31). The position of table and floor lamps can work very effectively to stimulate stagnant energy in a house or workplace—lamps are often used in the southern part of the building to stimulate the acknowledgment and fame area of your life.

A light or flagpole may be incorporated in your garden to balance any irregular shaping of your house and give it a sense of symmetry. Light is an extremely useful and effective feng shui cure, and can be incorporated in the garden in the form of garden lighting (see page 96), or as objects that reflect light, such as shiny metal balls that can be tucked in among the plants, mirrors that can be hung from the fence, and even water surfaces.

■ FOR **LIVING ROOM**, SEE **FAMILY OR LIVING ROOM** ON PAGES 84–85.

■ FOR **LOCATION**, SEE **IDEAL HOME AND LOCATION** ON PAGES 110–111.

LOW PRODUCTIVITY PROTECTION

Low productivity and low morale seem to go hand in hand. It might be wise to work out the lucky orientation of each member of your staff (see pages 122–123). Working in a building that resonates for only some staff members can cause enormous difficulties and clashes. Also, check the elemental orientation between staff members, supervisors, and managers. Solutions for people who are not naturally compatible can be found on pages 56–58.

If a member of your workforce is feeling particularly hostile, there are two important things that you need to check to help make that person feel more comfortable. First, determine whether his entrance into the building should be changed. Ideally, the owner of the business and staff members should enter the building through the main entrance to encourage beneficial energy to circulate through the building. However, if the orientation of the entrance is not aligned with that of an individual, then alternative possibilities should be investigated, such as using a side entrance.

Second, make sure that the affected person's desk is facing one of his lucky directions (see pages 122–123). Also check for the following feng shui problems:

• Are there any poison arrows aimed at your workforce members when they are sitting at their desks? If so, shield them from the poison arrow by placing a potted plant or another feng shui cure in front of the object causing the disturbance (see pages 26–27).

• Are they sitting with their backs to the entrance to their workplace? If so, move them so they are facing the entrance.

• Are they sitting at the end of a long corridor? If so, relocate them so that they are sitting in a position where the energy is allowed to meander gracefully to them.

LUCKY DIRECTIONS AND AREAS

WHAT IS YOUR LUCKY DIRECTION?

Good fortune, an increased salary, job promotion, and general happiness at work can be stimulated in your favor if you place your desk so that it faces a compass direction favorable to you.

Each person has either an easterly or westerly orientation and this gives him or her four compass directions that are personally favorable. Follow the directions on pages 58–59 to determine your orientation. Go to pages 184–185 to check that you have done your calculations correctly.

If your orientation is east, then the following directions are favorable:

• East • Southeast • South • North

For example, a man born in 1963 would have an eastern orientation. He would then experience a good flow of beneficial energy at work if his desk and the entrance to his workplace were facing east. However, a woman born in 1963 would have a western orientation and would benefit from having her desk facing west.

If your orientation is west, then the following directions are favorable:

• West • Northwest • Southwest • Northeast

By placing your bed, desk, or favorite chair so that it faces the direction favorable to you, you will attract beneficial energy into your life. You will find that if you sit at your desk or stand at your workstation with your back facing any of your lucky directions, you can concentrate better and will be able to enhance your good fortune. If you place your bed in a position where your head is pointing in your lucky direction, you will find that you will be able to sleep more soundly and restfully.

WHERE ARE YOUR LUCKY AREAS?

Your house or place of business has areas that are particularly lucky for you. It is important that you spend the majority of your time in your lucky areas. If you do not, you may feel uncomfortable in your house or workplace and experience demotion, unhappy relationships, or accidents. You can also burglarproof the windows and doors in unlucky areas, as they are more susceptible to break-ins. It is particularly important that your bedroom is in a lucky area so you have restful sleep and that your desk or any other area where you spend a lot of time is also in a lucky area, for maximum productivity.

To determine which areas in your house or place of business are lucky for you, take a piece of paper and trace the grid and numbers below—this is the luo-shu square. Make a plan of your house, garden, or workplace and figure out where the compass directions fall. Align the luo-shu square over your plan.

If you are of a western orientation, numbers 2, 6, 7, and 8 are favorable and relate respectively to the compass directions of southwest, northwest, west, and northeast. On your grid, shade in these squares to indicate your lucky areas. The unshaded areas (indicated by blue coloring in the illustration below left) are your unlucky areas. Shade the corresponding areas on your house, garden, or workplace plan.

If you are of an eastern orientation, numbers 1, 3, 4, and 9 are favorable directions and relate respectively to the compass directions of north, east, southeast, and south. On your grid, shade these squares to indicate your lucky areas. The unshaded areas (indicated by blue coloring in the illustration below right) are the unlucky areas. Shade the corresponding areas on your house, garden, or workplace plan.

Calculate the lucky and unlucky areas for all your family members or work colleagues. Find out the personal orientation of each person by using the system described on pages 58–59. To figure out if you are compatible with your home or workplace, see pages 136–137.

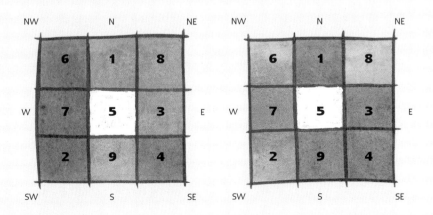

M

MAKING AMENDS AND KEEPING THE PEACE

There are some invaluable feng shui cures that can be used to help you repair a poor flow of energy or communication with your spouse and to help keep the peace with your neighbors.

If you have been experiencing a rough patch in your marriage or relationship, tie your wedding rings together with a red ribbon and hang them on the headboard in the master bedroom for seventy days. The red ribbon will help to stabilize the energy in your marriage or relationship. If you do not have wedding rings, consider placing a carved wooden images of a turtle on either side of your bed on the bedside tables. Turtles are important images of longevity, which you can evoke for your relationship.

If the male partner is unhappy in the relationship, consider removing any water features from the left-hand or yin side of the house (as you are standing at the front door looking in). Also, remove or cover any mirrors in the master bedroom and/or in the bedroom that you share. A mirror in the bedroom shared by a couple symbolizes a third person in the relationship.

Sometimes, conflict with your neighbors can occur because there are poison arrows generated by both your properties. Even if your neighbor does not believe in feng shui principles, use your knowledge not only to screen the poison arrows emanating from your neighbor's property but also to shield the poison arrows

---

FENG SHUI TIP

Some practitioners believe that if there are problems between neighbors, the *xiaoren*, or little people, may be to blame. To exorcise their mischievous presence, have a noisy housewarming party (remember to invite your neighbors!) to drive the little people away.

---

directed at your neighbor's property from your side of the fence (see pages 26–27).

If you notice that arguments with your neighbor occur in a particular area, check for poison arrows or stimulate a soothing feng shui cure such as implementing a water feature in that area.

MEETINGS

When making preparations for an important boardroom meeting, take some time to work out the seating arrangements. The person who is conducting the meeting or who is your key negotiator should be seated in what is called "the honored guest position," which is the chair most visible from the doorway. That person should also be facing one of her lucky directions (see pages 122–123).

Make sure the view from the chair is pleasant and does not include doorways to the bathroom. For a very important meeting, place a screen and some potted plants in the room facing the entrance to the boardroom, to shield the person who must sit with her back to the door.

The boardroom table should be in proportion to the boardroom and should be made of hardwood. One auspicious height for such a table is thirty-one inches. The table must accommodate an even number of people, and only an even number of attendees should be invited to the meeting. To generate friendly relations, the tabletop must be circular, oval, or octagonal. In feng shui, square tables are not auspicious, as the poison arrows created by the sharp points of the corners can create arguments and may leave negotiations unresolved. If you have a square table, place a circular or octagonal centerpiece in the middle of the table to divert some of the poison arrows. Placing a large, round, decorative object, such as a crystal bowl, on the table will generate harmony and good communication.

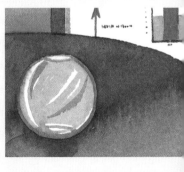

MENTORS AND TRAVEL ASPIRATION

The aspiration that governs the acquisition of friends, the support of influential people in authority, and the meeting of important people through your travels is governed by northwesterly energy. If you feel you are surrounded by unscrupulous people at work or are staying in one place for too long, you may wish to stimulate the flow of energy in the mentor/travel area of your house or workplace. This energy is also helpful for people seeking spiritual help and succor.

If you would like to increase your chances of meeting more helpful people or traveling, include wind chimes in that section of your home or workplace. You may also include your stereo system somewhere in the room. Do not play the music too loudly, as harsh sounds tend to disrupt the flow of beneficial qi. Apart from traditional feng shui cures, you can also do good deeds for others to help kick-start the flow of energy in this area.

To attract powerful supporters of your family or business, you should hang a bagua over the entrance to your home or office. Also, focus on your living or family room or staff room. Position a floor lamp in the northwestern section of this room and leave the lamp switched on for at least a couple of hours a day.

Another way of activating a particular area of your home or place of business is to incorporate something that resonates with your personal element. To determine your element, see pages 56–57. The table below provides some suggestions for objects you could include in your mentor area to enhance your good fortune.

If your windows in this area face a gloomy aspect or an unattractive view, such as a brick wall, use attractive, richly colored drapes, preferably with swags and a generous amount of material, to

YOUR ELEMENT	OBJECTS FOR THE MENTORS AREA
Earth	A brown or ocher-colored ceramic wall plate.
Metal	Metal wind chimes.
Wood	A drawing or a picture of a powerful person.
Water	Clear bowl with colorful marbles or glass chips filled with water with a lighted floating candle.
Fire	As objects of the Fire element should be avoided in this area, include something from an element supportive of you—Earth.

balance the yin nature of the windows. For the mentor area, try to incorporate some yellow or gold into the color scheme of the curtains or use colorful tassels to hold back the curtains from the window.

Also include objects that reflect the light in this area, such as clear rock crystals, glass ornaments, or mirrors. Use a mirror in this area if it can be positioned to reflect a pleasant outlook, either internally or externally. Also include pictures of people enjoying themselves, and incorporate some yellow or gold with the curtains or use gold- or yellow-colored tassels as tiebacks for the curtains or as window decoration.

In the northwestern section of your garden, you may wish to plant a garden that will flower at the beginning of winter, as this direction corresponds with winter. This kind of garden will need to include a number of frost-resistant plants, such as certain evergreens and bulbs. Include objects of metal or stone—perhaps statues of spiritual leaders, such as the Buddha, Jesus Christ, the Virgin Mary, and the holy saints, or of mentors, such as Roman senators or Greek philosophers. Also consider scattering some reflective silver- or gold-colored pebbles among the plants to evoke an atmosphere of success.

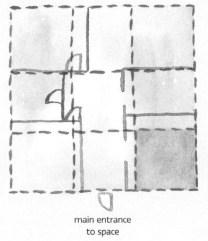

mentors/friends corner

main entrance to space

MIRRORS

A FENG SHUI CURE

Mirrors are exceptionally useful feng shui tools, especially for manipulating the flow of energy in the house. Flat mirrors can be used to stimulate energy in the fame and acknowledgment area. However, if your fame and acknowledgment area is in your bedroom, do not place a mirror there. It is considered most unlucky to have a mirror in the bedroom.

You may wish to use a mirror above your front door to keep it clear of any negative qi. Although a flat mirror will work, it is best to use a convex mirror to diffuse the negative energy more efficiently, as it distorts the image—and thus disperses the energy—rather than simply reflecting the image.

Mirrors can be positioned on your walls so that they reflect a pleasant aspect, preferably from outside your house. This is a cheap way to bring more of the garden or nature into the building. It is important not to allow two mirrors to be positioned on opposite walls so that they reflect each other.

In feng shui, mirrors positioned symmetrically on each of two walls that meet as a protruding corner can effectively negate the poison arrow that would normally be created by that corner.

Mirrors can also be used to "mask" an entire area. For example, if your bathroom and toilet are not auspiciously placed—if they are positioned in the wealth sector of the house or can be seen from the front door—you can place a mirror on the toilet or bathroom door to "hide" the room from sight.

Be careful with your placement of mirrors, as they are very powerful tools for moving energy about. Placing a mirror directly in front of the entrance to your home or garden, for instance, is believed to deflect the movement of the energy directly out of the area, which can lead to a sense of stagnation and disharmony in that area.

potted plant

mirrors on both walls to create the desired projection symbolically

MOVEMENT

A FENG SHUI CURE

SEE ALSO **PETS: A FENG SHUI CURE** ON PAGE 141.

Mobiles, whirligigs, weather vanes, flags, and other flexible objects that move with the flow of the wind deflect poison-arrow energy and encourage beneficial energy through your home or place of business.

If your bathroom is windowless, tie a red ribbon to the ventilation grill to alleviate the potential stagnation of energy in the room. Place a mobile or whirligig in the corners of a room to dissipate the stagnation of energy. These types of objects should be made of natural materials, such as handmade paper or wood.

The stagnant energy in corners can also be dissipated by burning incense in each corner of the room. Choose an incense stick that contains good-quality ingredients and avoid incense that contains a lot of chemicals or is based on dung.

Mobiles should be placed where they will move slightly in the breeze, such as in front of a ventilation grille or outside on a sheltered balcony. If your mobile falls down in the breeze, consider using another cure in that area—perhaps hang a crystal on the inside of a nearby window.

A weather vane should be used if you can see the sharp edge of a neighboring roofline pointed toward your building. The movement of the weather vane will deflect the poison-arrow energy made by the sharp angles of your neighbor's house.

Consider using mobiles and other similar remedies in the northern part of your home to stimulate your career, or in the southwest to add a bit more fun and lightheartedness to your relationship, especially if you and your partner have been experiencing very strong emotions (either positive or negative).

If you are sitting or sleeping under a beam, consider placing a banner or flags along the beam. If you sit under a beam and cannot move your chair or desk elsewhere, hang a mobile immediately above your head. This will help to disperse any negative energy that was descending upon you and possibly causing headaches, stress, or feelings of anger.

O

OFFICE CLUTTER

UNCLUTTERING STRATEGIES

With the advent of computers in modern-
day business, it was thought that paperless
business practices would soon evolve.
Strangely enough, this did not happen, and
we seem to have as much paper now as we
did before.

When you are planning the uncluttering
of your office, you will need to use certain
strategies, such as regularly going through
your files and assessing the currency of the items and whether you
need to keep them to comply with any legal requirements or
because of certain industry practices. You will also need to
determine whether they can—or should—be stored in an off-site
facility, or how they can be stored on site in such a way as to be
accessible and easy to update.

However, before you start sorting your papers, you need places to
store them, such as expanding files with labels, hanging file folders
and their metal frames, and filing cabinets. Before filing, refiling, or
consolidating your documents, devise a strategy for screening
information and decide on a consistent method of figuring out
where to file the paper. Do not have a "sort later" pile—this file is

---

FENG SHUI TIP

Is work slow or are there no new contracts coming in? The
answer to this dilemma is to clear your desk whenever you finish
work, and, in particular, to leave the central area free of any
clutter. By doing this, you are symbolically setting up an empty
space so that new work can come your way.

---

notorious for growing bigger and bigger until it becomes unmanageable. File immediately.

Business files can be organized by subject matter, and the material inside your files can be arranged in either alphabetical, geographic, or date order. There are many types of business file categories, such as:

- Central files and work files (the latter are the files necessary for the day-to-day running of your business)
- Staff files, including job descriptions, employees' contact details, résumés, certificates, diplomas and related credentials, and professional memberships
- Legal staff requirements, such as general guidelines, safe work practices, policies, and procedures
- Legal business requirements, such as relevant industry practice guidelines and registration documents
- Financial papers, such as bills to be paid, bankbooks and statements, checkbooks and statements, credit card statements, insurance policies, investment papers, payment books, and tax statements
- Job manuals and information
- Trade literature, design guides, and tender information
- Professional and work-related information, journals, and articles
- Competitors' details and information
- Information about forthcoming trade fairs, conferences, and seminars

With all your information filed appropriately and easy to retrieve, you will save valuable time and therefore increase your productivity. Another way of keeping clutter at bay is by keeping your desk clear of paper, using a tray system to keep track of your personal workload. A tray system can be as simple or as complex as is needed. It needs to be placed at the first port of call in any business and should be easily accessible—within arm's reach. Simple in and out trays can be established.

Consider having a "pending" tray for work to be completed within one or two days. Also include a tray for weekly and monthly tasks, as well as for "reading," "filing," and "receipts."

OFFICE PLAN

Open-plan or general offices are spaces where two or more people work in the same room. Semiprivate offices divided by screens can also be considered open-plan. Particular attention must be paid to the placement of desks and chairs in these types of offices.

It is important that the office space, whether in an individual or general office, is a regular shape with no protruding corners, as these create poison arrows that can hit other staff members. If a person is in the line of a poison arrow, his work will suffer, with symptoms ranging from a high absentee rate to an inability to meet deadlines or come up with new ideas (see pages 26–27 for ways to deflect poison arrows).

With seating, it is important that staff members are made to feel comfortable. The first step is to protect them from poison arrows and the second is to make sure that they are not seated with their backs to a door or an opening in their cubicles.

Corridors between cubicles, offices, and general office space conduct qi through the various spaces and openings. For qi to

benefit you, you must be seated so that you are facing the point at which the qi enters. If you sit with your back to an opening, you will feel as if you are in danger and may consequently feel defensive and suffer from low morale. Positioning a desk against a wall is also inauspicious because there is very little space for the qi to flow in front of the person at the desk.

In a general office, desks should not be placed facing each other. This is a confrontational arrangement and leads to bickering and arguments. It is best to place desks in an octagonal arrangement. If you

DIRECTION	ENERGY
North	Motivated and successful
South	Relaxed and comfortable
East	Charismatic and authoritative
West	Inventive and efficient

use this formation, make sure the desks all have rounded corners so that poison arrows are not created by sharp angles on the desktops.

Be wary of having your desk positioned at the end of a long, straight corridor or near the bottom of a staircase. Hang wind chimes to slow down energy that rushes along a corridor or flight of stairs. Choose wind chimes that sound melodious, as they can attract prosperous energy into the building, whether they are made from metal or wood.

In an individual office, it is still important to position the desk correctly if you want to advance in your business and/or your job. Do not sit with your back to the office door. The optimum position for your desk is the corner diagonally opposite the door.

Check the proportions of your desk and make sure your chair is in proportion with it, and comfortable. In feng shui, there are auspicious and inauspicious measurements for important pieces of furniture and for office windows and doors (see page 87).

You may also like to align your desk with one of your lucky directions (see pages 122–123) to encourage certain types of energy.

FENG SHUI TIP

If you are in an open-plan office, it is best if you sit in a position (preferably in the southeast) so that you do not see the backs of your colleagues. If you cannot change the position of your desk, consider making a symbolic fence around you by, for example, placing a plant or filing cabinet on the side of your desk and getting a chair with a high back (symbolic of supportive mountains at your back).

OFFICE WARMING

Many Chinese businesses begin their life with an office-warming ceremony, to ensure their success and prosperity. Such ceremonies have been developed in feng shui to clear the space of any negative energy attached to it, and then attract beneficial qi to the workspace.

The ceremony combines a cleansing of the business space with the lighting of a small, contained fire to symbolize the entry of the cosmic breath of the dragon—in other words, beneficial energy—into the office or business space.

In the Chinese culture, the time of birth is very important for figuring out whether a baby will be lucky or unlucky in life. Lucky and unlucky days and times can be determined by consulting the *Tong Shu,* or Chinese almanac. Similarly, the hour when a business begins its operation can have an effect on the general flow of clients to the business, which symbolizes the flow of beneficial energy to it.

The first step toward the ceremony is working out the lucky day and time for the commencement of your business at the new premises. Consult either the *Tong Shu* or a feng shui practitioner to ascertain the precise hour your business should open. There are many lucky days and times during the year, so all you need to do is choose the one closest to the day you are thinking of commencing your business.

Once the date and time have been set, work at getting everything ready for the start of business, clean and outfit the new premises,

---

FENG SHUI TIP

If you travel a lot, hang a gray tassel in the northwest section of your home or workplace to ensure a safe journey, or carry with you a two-inch Chinese coin with the inscription "Wish you safe wherever you go." When staying at a hotel, hang a natural crystal in the window and lightly spray your own perfume or aftershave in the room to clear stagnant energies.

and get stock. Once you have finished setting up your space (preferably the day before the ceremony), tape black paper, cardboard, or cloth on all openings to the workspace, such as the doors, windows, and air vents. Switch off all electrical appliances at least one hour before the ceremony.

When ready, gather all your staff outside the main entrance to the workspace.

Place a red sash or banner across the main entrance (preferably in the upper section or above the door), and light a small fire in a cauldron half-filled with sand, or on a low, movable charcoal stove. Stoke the fire. Assign one of your employees to be the timekeeper, and ask her to alert you when the auspicious time for the start of your business approaches.

At the correct moment, place the cauldron or stove at the front entrance, right under the lintel, and carefully step over it, leading with your left foot. Each employee should then enter the premises by stepping over the fire, also leading with the left foot.

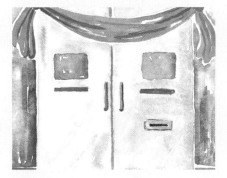

At this point, take down the red banner from the doorway, remove the black coverings, and start the electrical appliances. Celebrate with music and a party. This will harmonize well with the nature-magic tradition of sharing food to symbolize the bonding of a group of people.

Remember that you can consult a feng shui practitioner, or ask one to be on hand, to help guide you through this simple ritual.

ORIENTATION

To determine if your home or workplace has an eastern or western orientation, you can use a standard Western compass. The best way to figure out your building's orientation is to determine its sitting direction—that is, the compass direction in which the back of the building faces.

In offices that are part of a larger commercial building, it is important to know the sitting direction of the building where your office is and the relationship of your office to the building. For instance, your office building may be sitting in the west, while the main entrance to your office faces toward the back of the building. The sitting position of your office is still in the west, even though the main entrance of your office faces the building's sitting position.

If the building is sitting in the following compass directions, its orientation is to the east:

• East • Southeast • South • North

If the building is sitting in the following compass directions, its orientation is to the west:

• West • Northwest • Southwest • Northeast

To find your building's orientation using a compass, stand with your back against the back wall of the building (the wall as far back from the main entrance as possible). Align your compass to the north and then read the compass grade to determine which way the back of the building is facing. Use the table opposite to find out what your compass grade means.

HOW COMPATIBLE ARE YOU WITH YOUR HOUSE?

Do the calculations on pages 58–59 to work out your personal orientation number and whether you are of an eastern or western orientation. Now find out if your house has an eastern or western orientation (see opposite page).

In apartments, it is important to figure out the sitting direction of the building that contains your apartment and the relationship of your apartment to the building. For instance, if the back of your apartment building faces north and the front door of your apartment faces the back of the building, your sitting position is still to the north, even though what you would think of as the front of your apartment is facing north.

To feel relaxed and safe in your home, your house's orientation should ideally match your own. If you live in a house that has an opposite orientation to your own, you may experience arguments, illness, unhappiness in friendships and other relationships, as well as demotion in your career and accidents. However, there are ways of counterbalancing the negative energy flow, for example, by changing your main entry into your home so that the direction is more suitable to you or changing your bedroom so that it is situated in one of your lucky areas (see pages 122–123).

DO YOU SUIT YOUR WORKPLACE?

Do the calculations on pages 58–59 to determine your orientation number and whether you are of an eastern or western orientation. Now do the calculations on page 136 to find out if your workplace has an eastern or western orientation (see opposite page).

Sometimes it can be difficult to get an accurate compass reading at the back of the workplace. This can be due to a number of reasons, such as electrical interference. If this is the case, go to the front of the building and take a compass reading. If you still cannot get a reading, go inside the building and take the measurement facing the main entrance or with your back to the back entrance.

If you are not compatible with your workplace, do not despair. This knowledge may help you to understand why you may be having some trouble at, or dissatisfaction with, your work. To remedy such incompatibility, consider one of three options:

• Set up a home office.
• Make sure that your desk is facing one of your four favorable directions (see pages 122–123).
• Find an entrance to the building that is facing one of your four favorable directions and use this instead of the main entrance.

COMPASS GRADE	SITTING DIRECTION
22.5°–67.5°	Northeast
67.5°–112.5°	East
112.5°–157.5°	Southeast
157.5°–202.5°	South
202.5°–247.5°	Southwest
247.5°–292.5°	West
292.2°–337.5°	Northwest
337.5°–22.5°	North

P

PATHS, PAVEMENTS, AND DRIVEWAYS

Assess all the paths in your garden and soften any straight
outlines—feng shui says that energy flows beneficially in curves
and detrimentally in straight lines. To assure yourself that
changing the shape of your path is a very important step toward
creating a harmonious garden, one that is good for your soul
and the progress of your life, make a note of what happens at
the end of a straight path.

In particular, answer the following questions about your straight
path. If you answer "yes" to any of the questions, make reshaping
the straight path a priority in your gardening schedule. Is there:

1 Clutter or garden debris?
2 A dead or dying plant?
3 A garden structure in poor repair?
4 A tendency for arguments and disagreements to flare up?

There are many types of paths—concrete, brick, wood, gravel, and
grass, for example. Generally, in Western garden design, it is
believed that only one type of path should be used in the garden, to
give a sense of unity to the design. In the East, garden paths are
usually filled with a mixture of different types of materials.

One of the cheapest and most useful types of path is one filled
with gravel. Gravel paths allow some flexibility in terms of
changing and rearranging your garden—you can easily expand
garden beds and create paths that lead to newly cultivated sites, for
instance. Although gravel paths require maintenance, such as
raking and occasional weeding, they have a security benefit, as
walking on them creates a great deal of noise.

If you wish to be adventurous in your garden design, you could
consider choosing the materials for your paths according to the
direction each path is traveling in. For instance, a path that leads to
a garden shed situated in the north of your garden corresponds to

the element of Water, which is nurtured by Metal. Use a series of white, circular stepping-stones for this path.

Apart from the shape and material of the path, remember that the aspect of the path, the look of it as you move along it, must always be pleasant. Even if a path is curved, still consider planting low-growing shrubs and fragrant flowers and herbs along it to encourage the energy to flow beneficially. Fragrant herbs, such as lavender, rosemary, and thyme, are popular edgings. You could also experiment with using metal, wood, or another material to edge the path so that it is distinctly separate from the rest of the garden but still corresponds to the direction it is heading in. This principle can also be applied to the edging of garden beds situated in a particular compass direction.

Driveways are also strong channels of energy. If the driveway is long and straight, it will concentrate too much yang energy toward the house. Soften the edges of the driveway with garden shrubs and trees that have shallow roots, so they do not interfere with the driveway's surface. If you are constructing a driveway, design one that either gently curves between the front boundary line and the garage door or that curves in a horseshoe shape from the street, past your front door, and out to the street again.

DIRECTION	CORRESPONDING ELEMENT AND COLOR	CORRESPONDING TYPE OF PATH	CORRESPONDING GARDEN EDGING
Center Southwest Northeast	Earth Yellow and brown	Gravel, brick, or stone paving	Brick, stone, or molded terra-cotta edgings
West Northwest	Metal White and silver	White gravel, brick, or stone paving	Brick, stone, or pressed metal edgings
North	Water Blue and black	Bluestone paving	Pressed metal edgings
East Southeast	Wood Green	Decking, brick, or stone	Wood, brick, or stone edgings
South	Fire Red	Decking	Wood edgings

PERSONAL CLUTTER

UNCLUTTERING STRATEGIES

Clutter around you can sometimes indicate that you have not wished to focus on yourself or your direction in life. However, it is worth trying to remove the clutter around you—you have many excellent qualities, and the clues to your life's purpose are embedded in the clutter.

One of the most important issues to look into is your sense of identity. To figure out what kind of person you are, before clearing and analyzing the clutter, make a list of what you think you like and don't like. If this feels too difficult, try making a list for a hero or heroine of a story, and imbue him or her with all your likes and dislikes in terms of clothing styles, colors, shoes, socks and stockings, perfume or aftershave, jewelry, and accessories.

We often have things that were given to us by friends and relatives, and these may indicate how they view us. Sometimes these objects are well off the mark when compared with how we perceive ourselves. If there are items that do not suit your self-image, consider discarding them or giving them away, unless the item was clearly given with love and care.

FENG SHUI TIP

Uncluttering may help you to find a partner, either in business or in a personal relationship, once you have made space for that person to come into your life or business. Sandra had been single for some time, and had decided to use feng shui to help her find a mate. She was advised to clear out her bedroom and bathroom. Sandra cleared clothing from her closet and left it half empty, and cleaned out her bathroom. By doing this, she made room for someone to enter her life. Several weeks later she met a man and they have been together ever since.

PETS

A FENG SHUI CURE

SEE ALSO **FISH TANKS** ON PAGE 88.

Pets are well known for their ability to circulate energy around the house and are helpful in relieving stress. They can also help to enhance the wealth area of your house or place of business (see pages 18–21).

You can position their beds or feeding bowls so that the animals will go through the wealth sector (in the southeastern part of your house) to reach them. Build a kennel for your dog, a roomy cage for your rabbit, or plant a patch of catnip for your cat in the southeastern part of your garden to generate good luck in your finances.

It is auspicious to have two pets, preferably one female (yin) and one male (yang), and to allow them to play at random throughout the house (after some suitable house training!), as animals have a natural tendency to flow with the energy and focus on troublesome spots. Watch the movement of your older animals to see which areas they like and which they avoid—this is a good indication of energy problems. Young cats, in particular, appear to thrive on helping you clear your clutter by, for instance, disturbing mounds of accumulated material.

Getting young animals is also a great encouragement to clear the house of clutter. However, if their energy becomes too yang (overly stimulated), consider giving them a dark blue collar to help balance their high spirits with yin (passive) energy—or, better still, take them for a walk or let them go outside for a short period of time.

If you can't afford the time or money to have a pet, consider planting a tree or shrub that encourages butterflies or birds into the garden. To attract birds, plant such trees as acacias, birches, crab apples, figs, firs, oaks, pines, and spruces. Also consider planting shrubs and flowers such as fuchsias, honeysuckles, and geraniums. To attract butterflies, plant daffodils, lavender, rhododendrons, or rosemary.

PLANTS, TREES, AND HEDGES

In feng shui, plants, trees, and hedges are very useful in screening either poison arrows created by features in the environment, garden, or structures, or unfavorable energy created by inauspicious views from your house, or any other inauspicious features in your garden.

Overall, fragrant trees and hedges, or those with attractively colored leaves or flowers, are the best types of plants for screening negative energy of any sort. One kind of attractive hedge can be made with a repeated planting of abelia, camellia, hibiscus, honeysuckle, and orange jasmine. However, make sure the screening plants on your front boundary line do not grow higher than three feet in height. Otherwise, qi will not flow as beneficially.

The shape of plants can attract certain types of energy into a garden and into your life. Use the table below to see the correspondences between plant shapes, compass directions, and the five Chinese elements.

Each type of plant shape can be used in the corresponding direction in the garden to enhance the flow of the energy from that particular direction. This is particularly useful if you have a blockage of energy from a certain direction. For instance, if the view is unpleasant from your easterly direction, blocking energy that attracts culture and wisdom, use rectangular plants. To achieve a sense of harmony, health, and balance in a home and garden, it is imperative to balance the energies of all the elements.

DIRECTION	ELEMENT	SHAPES AND LINES
Center/Southwest/Northeast	Earth	Square
West/Northwest	Metal	Circle
North	Water	Undulating line
East/Southeast	Wood	Rectangle
South	Fire	Triangle

However, it is also important to choose a way of enhancing beneficial energy from a particular direction. If some of the plants suggested will not thrive in a certain direction in your garden, consider incorporating one of the many feng shui cures and other garden feng shui strategies, such as planting flowers or shrubs that flower in a color that corresponds to the elemental energy you wish to attract.

To enhance the flow of energy from the southwest or northeast, which corresponds to the flow of stable and life-enhancing qi, plant square plants such as yew trees, use a garden edging of boxwood, or fill a garden bed with California poppies or verbena. To harness the flow of energy from the west and northwest, plant circular plants such as hydrangeas and chives. Rounded shapes also manifest in some trees—the oak tree, for instance, and weeping plants of various varieties, such as the willow. To encourage the flow of energy from the east and southeast, plant rectangular plants such as dogwood and certain cypresses.

To enhance the flow of energy from the south, which is believed to be lucky, plant triangular plants, such as beeches, some evergreen conifers (do not plant trees that will eventually be very large and block the flow of this energy), ferns, and irises. To enhance the flow of nurturing energy from the north, plant trees and shrubs that have undulating or wavy shapes, such as honeysuckle, wisteria, and rhododendrons.

FENG SHUI TIP

Keep trees at a distance from the house to avoid root damage to the building, which may lead to corresponding cracks occurring in the occupants' lives. Ideally, trees should be planted at such a distance that they do not cast a shadow on the house when they are fully matured. For example, if a tree grows to a height of twenty-six feet, plant it twenty-six feet from the house.

PURSES, WALLETS, AND BAGS

UNCLUTTERING STRATEGIES

The state of your bag, purse, or wallet is an indication of the state of your wealth, and of your ability to manifest wealth in your life. An overstuffed wallet full of receipts relating to money long gone and credit card payments that have left you in some financial distress is an indication that you do not feel able to move forward in gaining wealth.

When you next have to wait somewhere for a while, such as in a doctor's waiting room or a dentist's office, instead of reading a magazine, clean out your purse and wallet. Arrange your money in order of denomination—this way you will know at a glance how much you really have. Sort through all your credit cards, discount cards, and store cards, and decide which ones you really need to carry.

In feng shui, the wealth aspiration corresponds to the elements of Wood and Water. If you are at home, take your purse or wallet and clear out everything—money, cards, written paper scraps, receipts, business cards—everything.

FENG SHUI TIP

A massing of plants in the southeast segment of the garden will help to correct the flow of energy to your finances. There are even particular plants that are believed to bring good luck in your wealth sector, such as clumping golden bamboo—because of its similarity to the color of gold, it is believed to encourage the flow of wealth to the owner of the garden. Bamboo is also symbolic of strength and longevity; growing it at the back of your property will stimulate a nurturing energy in your life. Include a piece of bamboo in your purse or wallet to stimulate your financial security. Other plants that encourage prosperity include the jade or money tree (*Portulacaria afra*) with its coin-shaped leaves, and the large, green perforated-leaf monstera (*Monstera deliciosa*), which needs to be planted in a sheltered area, preferably in the southeast area of the garden.

Do not sort anything at this stage. Use a damp cloth to clean the lint and dust from the purse or wallet, and burn a stick of incense to activate new energy to enter the purse or wallet (as well as your own financial matters) and clear out stagnant energy.

You may want to place in your purse or wallet a small picture of a tranquil water scene, for instance, or a picture of a beautifully appointed beachside resort with clear blue skies and palm trees, indicating an intention to retire early and prosperously. Do not choose pictures of storms, or atmospheric but gloomy seascapes, or sunsets over the water—these pictures will not enhance prosperous energy.

For those who have bags, the contents can be an easy indication of the state of your life. If your bag is overflowing with stuff, representing the many things you tend to do in a day, uncluttering your bag and figuring out what you do and don't need will lead to a similar uncluttering in your life.

If you have too many bags, consider throwing out or giving away those that cannot be matched to your shoes (depending on the fashion) and your clothes.

If you work at home or if you have a secure office, consider placing your uncluttered purse or wallet on the wealth sector of your desk. Or simply place a feng shui coin in your uncluttered purse or wallet to generate a flow of good luck to that part of your life.

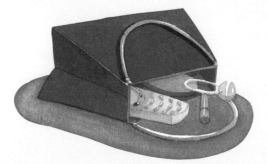

RECEPTION AREA

The reception area must be well positioned and decorated to enhance the full potential of your business, because it is the first area to receive the enhancing qi energy. It is important that the area is designed to encourage the flow of energy through to the rest of the building and that any potentially harmful poison arrows are blocked.

The person at the reception desk is essential to the organization. He or she has been employed to present a welcoming and efficient persona to clients and gives a very important first impression to people approaching the business. It is imperative that the receptionist is not sitting directly opposite the main entrance. This is because the qi rushes in through the main entrance and hits the reception desk, giving the receptionist a sense of unease and causing lack of focus, as well as a predisposition to headaches. This is intensified if a poison arrow is also pointing at the receptionist.

Poison arrows are often caused by sharp design features of neighboring buildings that aim arrows toward the main entrance, by a straight road leading directly to the main entrance, or by a tower or pole opposite it.

There are a number of ways of deflecting arrows outside the main entrance door (see pages 26–27), such as leaving a strong light on permanently at your main entrance. However, there are some

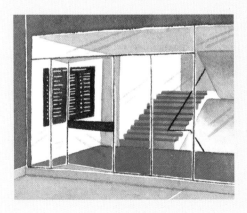

solutions that can be implemented within the reception area, such as placing pieces of rounded furniture and plants in front of the receptionist or installing a statue or sculpture that features gentle, curving lines. Rounded curves cause the energy to slow down, as it has to move around the object in its path.

You can deflect negative energy in a reception area by placing a mirror or a representation of the bagua mirror above the main entrance. To allow the energy to move further into the building, the reception area should have some curves that encourage the energy to flow around it and through to the work space behind.

Plants can be used to deflect architectural poison arrows, such as those created by columns and protruding corners, by being placed in front of the column or corner.  Plants can also be used to soften the rectangular outlines of some of the larger pieces of furniture in the reception area, by being placed by the corner.

Never allow your reception area to be a dark, overly yin room, as this can cause feelings of depression and unease. Place an even number of floor lamps that spread their light upward in the corners of the area and use potted plants with red, orange, or yellow flowers. Choose lamps that are well-rounded. Avoid light fittings and lamps with sharp, angular design elements.

FENG SHUI TIP

It is important to keep your indoor plants healthy and in contact with enough sunlight to prosper. To increase wealth in the business, consider placing a coin in the soil of your potted plant. Popular indoor plants for prosperity include the "money plant," also known as a *Dracaena*, an evergreen that thrives indoors. You may consider including indoor plants that have brightly colored yellow, orange, or red-hued flowers. These types of plants would be particularly beneficial near a window in a dark, yin room.

RELATIONSHIPS ASPIRATION

Feng shui principles can be successfully applied to attracting the energies of romance and love. Focus on the southwestern area of your home and your bedroom (see pages 18–21).

Check the colors and lighting used in your relationship area. Be careful to include a balance of cool and warm colors, and make sure there is a balance between furniture and space. Include bright, warmly colored throw rugs or cushions if you are in the courting stages of your relationship or if you wish to revitalize the romance in your life. Place certain crystals, particularly rose quartz, in the area, or more candles to increase light.

Try to have a pair of objects, pictures, or furniture for balance and as a symbol of the type of energy you wish for your life. For example, have two candles, two complementary pictures or paintings, or two armchairs arranged symmetrically. Do the same in your bedroom. You may include symbols of conjugal happiness, such as two entwined hearts, two ducks, or a picture of a peony.

In both your bedroom and the relationships area, display photographs of yourself and your partner or of happy couples. Make sure that they do not clutter the area. Keep this area clean. You may also wish to add a mobile or wind chime to help move any stagnant energy in this space. The burning of incense will also stimulate beneficial qi. Choose patchouli, musk, ylang ylang, or jasmine incense to generate a loving atmosphere.

Sometimes, people will experience trouble in their relationships if the area corresponding to the relationships aspiration is either missing or is a much smaller part of the house in relation to the rest of the aspirations. This may occur if your house is an irregular shape.

If the corner of a house that is supposed to represent the relationships aspiration is missing, square off the shape and mark the missing corner by planting a fruiting tree there or by installing a lamp in the garden. This will symbolically extend the missing segment of the house and strengthen your relationship aspiration.

Alternatively, plant a love garden, incorporating flowers and herbs traditionally associated with encouraging love, such as geranium, lavender, and lovage, in the missing section of the house.

If you cannot balance the corner from the outside, you can still balance it from the inside. If there are windows in the walls closest to the missing corner, hang a crystal in each window. If these walls create a protruding corner, prevent the corner from creating poison-arrow energy by placing a mirror on each side of the corner to create an illusion of an outward-pointing corner.

Also check the southwestern part of your garden. If you are feeling unloved or unhappy in a dead-end relationship, or have suffered a string of unsatisfying relationships, you can make changes in this aspect of your life by improving the relationships area of your garden. Reduce clutter in this part of the garden and use softening or screening strategies if this area of the garden is subject to poison arrows (see pages 26–27).

If you have been feeling lonely, check that this section of the garden is not too yin in energy. If this area is in constant shade and there is a sense of stagnation, your relationships may suffer from a similar feeling of ennui. Cut back any overgrowth and let more sunlight into this area to feel a marked improvement in this aspect of your life.

If the area is too yang (the garden beds are dry, there is not enough shade, or the ground is stony or arid, for instance), you may find that your relationships are too demanding and tiring. Plant more trees in this area to give shade, and perhaps add more mulch or humus to the soil.

Feng shui can be used to enhance your prospects of new love. Before attempting to enhance such prospects, you should unclutter and thoroughly clean your bedroom. Once you have cleared all negative energies by getting rid of the clutter and tidying your bed and closet or wardrobe, you will be able to enhance particular areas of your life by redecorating corresponding areas of your bedroom.

If you want to enhance your prospects of love, concentrate on the relationships corner in your bedroom (see pages 18–21).

To attract a new love, or to rekindle the flame of your existing relationship, follow these simple tips for decorating a bedroom:

1 Remove all pictures of yourself in which you are on your own.
2 Remove all empty jars and bottles.
3 Remove all pictures of, and objects given by, past partners in unhappy relationships.
4 Make sure there are even numbers of decorative objects such as candles, side tables, and pictures.
5 If you are buying furniture for your bedroom, consider dressing tables and chests of drawers that have even numbers of drawers.
6 Include special feng shui good luck symbols for love (see opposite).

Once you have located your relationship corner in the bedroom, use a bell or just clap your hands loudly in it to make sure that the area is clear of negative energy. Try to organize your furniture so that there is a flat surface in this corner that can be made into a small space devoted to attracting a relationship or enhancing your current relationship.

In this space, you could place a combination of the following feng shui good-luck symbols to improve your prospects for love:

FENG SHUI TIP

If you are planning an intimate dinner for two, clear your table of any previous negative associations by ringing a melodious bell over the table and the two chairs that you will be using for the meal. Walk around the table in a continuous circular motion and imagine all unhappiness from past relationships vanishing. Special feng shui decorations can be placed in the room where you are having dinner, such as a harmonious photograph showing both of you happy together or one of the most powerful feng shui cures to attract happiness and fidelity in a relationship—the composition of two duck figurines on a small, round mirror that comfortably accommodates them. The mirror symbolizes peaceful, calm waters.

- Two pieces of rose quartz of equal size
- A yang-colored cloth (reds, oranges, and pinks)
- A pair of red candles
- A picture of a pair of birds or butterflies (do not use actual dead butterflies)
- A floor lamp that is left switched on
- A yang-colored fan or a pair of flutes with red tassels hanging from one end
- Pictures of a pair of cranes or geese, symbolizing fidelity in marriage

Another thing to watch and "cure" is the presence of a beam over the bed. You may have troubles in your relationship if the beam runs above the bed in such a way that you sleep on one side and your partner sleeps on the other. However, arguments may be minimized (see pages 52–53) if you use a simple feng shui cure—a red ribbon tied across the beam, a banner of flags tied along the length of the beam (at least that part that hits the bed), two flutes (see page 86), or some wind chimes (see page 176).

REMOVING NEGATIVE ENERGY

If you or your family, your coworkers, or previous house owners or tenants have experienced anger, trauma, or sustained unhappiness in a space, consider requesting a feng shui practitioner with space-clearing experience to help to remove the negative energy left by these strong experiences. Alternatively, you may wish to carry out the following simple ritual yourself.

1 Find a bell that produces a sound melodious to your ear. Walk to the front door or main entrance of your premises, holding the clapper of your bell.

2 Take three deep breaths and imagine that you can feel the energy flowing through the front door. Imagine that you are caught in the energy flow as you wander in and out of all rooms of the building.

3 As you enter each room or area, feel or imagine seeing the flow of energy moving. If the energy in a particular room or area feels slow or seems to be disappearing, go to each corner of the room and clang the bell.

4 Listen to the sound of the bell. Imagine that the tiny vibrations of sound are stirring up the negative energy, detaching it from your space, and clearing it.

Be aware that, when these encoded energies are released, you may briefly experience an echo of the negative emotions or of the unhappy person's spirit. Remember that this is an echo only, and is not part of your current existence.

FENG SHUI TIP

Wear a small feng shui charm, such as a jade Bi, as protection from any stray negativity when doing a space clearing. A jade Bi is a round piece of jade with a hole in the middle. It may contain a coin or a Chinese good luck character. After the space clearing, you could hang the jade charm on the back of your front door to continue protecting your space from negative energy.

ROADS

In feng shui today, the movement of water in a river is equated
with the flow of traffic along the road outside your front door.
Traditionally, it was believed that living in an area where the streets
all ran parallel to each other in a grid formation caused bad feng
shui, but now only busy thoroughfares are believed to be
particularly bad feng shui.

Straight streets that do not have much traffic are not considered
a problem unless your house is situated at a T-intersection, at the
end of a dead-end street, or on the apex of a sharp bend.

It is best to avoid houses that have such strong energy flowing
directly at the house. However, it is possible to deflect the worst
of the energy by planting a hedge or constructing a fence. The
energy flowing along a roadway is too strong and is not beneficial,
becoming a poison arrow of negative energy.

Living on the corner of a street is also inauspicious, mainly
because the energy flowing past the front of your house is dispersed
by the energy flowing past your house on either side.

The ideal position is a meandering roadway or path that leads
past your front door in a gentle curve.

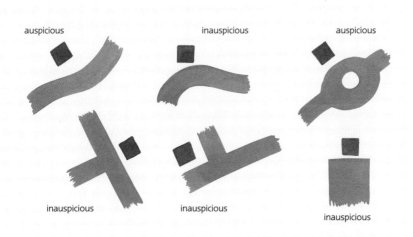

auspicious   inauspicious   auspicious

inauspicious   inauspicious

inauspicious

SHAPES AND FENG SHUI

The form school of feng shui believes that the shape of the
environment is very important for directing the right kind of qi
toward your home and business. According to ancient Chinese
mythology, four celestial beasts represent four aspects of the
environment, and it is important that a building is positioned
so the natural protection afforded by these beasts is activated
(see pages 22–23).

   Living or working on the top of a hill can make you feel
vulnerable to the elements and exposed to the harsher elements
of life, while living or working at the bottom of a hill may feel (and
in fact is) overwhelmingly dangerous, because the energy flowing
straight down the mountain will have created a poison arrow by the
time it hits the base of the mountain. Living or working on a flat

---

FENG SHUI TIP

Houses whose shape corresponds to the shape of their
environment are the most stable. However, for a prosperous
life, the following combinations are ideal:

• A house made of concrete and bricks (Earth) is best suited to
  mountainous terrain (Fire).
• A house with a corrugated roof or a large-scale metal
  skyscraper (Metal) is best situated near large bodies of water
  (Water).
• A house of irregular shapes and size (Water) is best suited to a
  rounded hillside or large-scale metal buildings (Metal).
• A house with wooden cladding or an apartment block (Wood) is
  best situated near large bodies of water (Water).
• A house with a sharp roofline (Fire) is best situated near a
  forest or skyscrapers (Wood).

---

area was traditionally considered inauspicious, but it is no longer thought to be problematic.

Balance and symmetry of shape are integral aspects of feng shui. Symmetry of shapes allows the optimal flow of energy within a property. Square-shaped properties and houses evoke the energy of the element of Earth, which is the most stable of energies.

Rectangles are symbolic of the energy of Wood, an energy believed to imbue the residents with a sense of growth and achievement, as well as flexibility and resilience. Square or rectangular houses, in terms of the floor plan, are considered most conducive to the best flow of qi, as they do not create sharp angles that make it difficult for qi to flow in and out.

A horseshoe-shaped house with a central courtyard at the front accepts the flow of qi more readily than one with a courtyard at the back.

Triangular-shaped houses and properties relate to the Fire element and can imbue an area with unstable energy, both wildly positive and dramatically negative. Although circular properties are rare, sometimes a house and garden are perched on a slightly domed hill; they will then attract the energy of Metal.

Irregularly shaped houses and properties are symbolic of the energy of Water. This leads to the generation of an unstable flow of qi, but it can be "cured" by disguising all the protruding corners as "garden rooms." If your house is not a regular shape, you can cure this by placing features in your garden, which extend the line of your house to make it symmetrical.

The position of your house on your plot of land is also important. On a square plot of land, the best position is right in the center, while on a rectangular plot, the house is best positioned near the front of the land.

It is important that the rooms of your house are a regular shape and that you use symmetry in your style of decoration. Particular problems occur in *L*-shaped rooms or rooms that have a prominent corner. This causes a poison arrow to pierce the interior and needs to be countered (see pages 26–27).

SHOES AND CLOTHING

UNCLUTTERING STRATEGIES

Sometimes, when we are feeling down, buying a nice pair of shoes or a beautiful dress can make us feel much better. However, if the dress or shoes do not suit the rest of our wardrobe, the feeling of pleasure does not remain for long, and soon we need

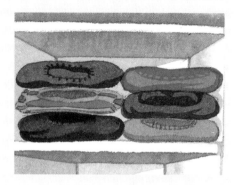

another "fix" to feel happy. This short-term stress solution can lead to long-term financial problems.

Knowing what clothing and shoes suit you, and being realistic about your body size and shape, will help you to unclutter your life. You may also decide to start a personal uncluttering journal (see page 165) in which you can paste all the pictures of clothing, makeup products and tips, fabric, jewelry, and other items that you like or feel are suitable for you. This will also help you to clear the clutter of magazines that you may have been loath to discard because there was a picture of an outfit you liked or a makeup tip you thought was useful. The journal will allow you to clear your room of unnecessary magazines while helping you to decide what you really like.

FENG SHUI TIP

Diane had a wardrobe full of clothes and many pairs of shoes, but still felt that she didn't have a thing to wear. In despair, she consulted a professional image consultant to determine, from her skin tone, what colors would suit her. The consultant also helped Diane find styles that would suit her body shape and frame and make her look slimmer. She threw or gave away all the clothes and shoes that did not suit her, and she found shopping a much easier and less expensive exercise, as she now knew what colors and styles flattered her. This made her feel good and in control.

To clear your clothing clutter, take out all your clothes and dump them onto your bed or a surface where you can easily sort through them. Assess whether the clothes are in good condition. Those that are in poor condition or are of poor quality should be thrown on a pile marked for immediate disposal or even recycled as cleaning rags.

Next, sort through the clothes that fit you at your current weight and shape.

We all have skinny, medium, and fat clothes. We sometimes hang onto clothes that symbolize when we were much thinner, theoretically providing us with a path to go back to those days. What this piece of clothing is really doing, however, is stagnating the energy around our self-image and making us feel uncomfortable about where we are now.

Remember that a piece of clothing will usually not, by itself, inspire you to lose weight or become fitter. Owning up to the shape you have now puts you a step closer to doing something about it, if you really feel uncomfortable about how you look. If these wrong-size pieces of clothing are in good condition, put them in a pile marked for your favorite charitable organization. It's often a good

idea to sort all your clothes into groups—suits, shirts, pants, skirts, sweats, coats, and jackets—to help you recognize the clothes you don't wear often. Often, the reason you do not wear a garment is because you have nothing that complements it.

To unclutter your collection of shoes, the first step is to throw out those shoes that are dated, scuffed, the wrong size, or blister your feet. The second step is to collect the shoes you feel uncomfortable in or that do not match any of your outfits. Put them in a box and consider having a party at which you can offer your friends their choice of the shoes and clothes you no longer need or want.

SOLID OBJECTS

A FENG SHUI CURE

Statues and other heavy objects are useful for slowing down fast-moving energy. They can be placed at the head or the base of a straight staircase, at the front door, or at the door leading into the reception area (if there is a straight path leading from the street to the front door or reception area). They will help positive energy to enter the building at a more graceful pace.

If the energy is channeled down a long, straight corridor, consider using a statue or large piece of furniture that does not have many sharp edges, such as a heavy wing chair, at the beginning or end of the corridor.

It is important that the heavy objects you use are rounded because this will encourage the energy to slow down in order to move around the object in its path. A round-edged table placed in a long hallway will slow the flow of energy. However, ensure that the large object is in proportion with the room; otherwise, the piece may take on a strong yang energy that will exacerbate the aggressively yang nature of the fast-moving qi that is going toward or past it.

If you are using a functional piece of furniture, such as a chair, make sure that you only use it for visitors (who should be allowed to sit in it for only a short duration) or decorative purposes. The strong energy striking the chair would not be conducive to relaxation.

Avoid Western statues that show a person or animal in distress or in anger—use statues and sculptures that give a sense of peace, balance, and harmony, such as a statue of Buddha. A popular variant is the statue of the Laughing Buddha, a fat, happy Buddha, which can be placed in the garden, facing the building, to attract abundance to the family or business.

Consider using statues and other heavy objects for stabilizing the creativity and children aspiration area of your house (see pages 15–19) or place of business.

SOUND

A FENG SHUI CURE

The sound of melodious music is a powerful way to stimulate positive energy and help it to flow through the house. Use music to clear negative, stagnant energy, particularly from the northwestern segment of the building, which corresponds to mentors and travel, or in the northeastern area, which relates to the knowledge aspiration.

Your sound system, television, or radio can be set up in these areas of the building to stimulate these aspects of your life. Ringing bells (see page 42) and using wind chimes (see page 176) are other, more traditional ways of using sound as a feng shui cure. Sound is also an excellent cure to use in an overly dark, shaded, yin room.

However, be wary about electrical sounds, such as the constant low-pitched whirring produced by machines that are switched on. Feng shui practitioners frown on keeping an electric clock near the bedside table and having a television or stereo in the bedroom. The sounds these appliances make (even when they are turned off) are believed to interfere with your rest because they constantly stimulate the energy in a room.

Televisions and stereos generate yang energy, so they are best kept in a cabinet or covered with a yin-colored cloth—this will rebalance their energy. If you are constantly at work in front of a computer screen, the sound of water will help to revitalize you.

You might choose one of the following tools to let sound clear your space:

- Five-rod wind chimes
- Gongs
- Drums (the Irish bodhrán, which is shaped like a tambourine and is hit with a stick, is a favorite with nature-magic practitioners)
- Tibetan cymbals
- Crystal singing bowls

You may also clear space by making your own sounds: Chant a mantra (a repeated phrase), clap your hands, or do a toning session. Toning is a technique that enables you to make sustained sounds of deep quality. Recordings of chants, tonings, and music for meditation are available commercially.

U

UNCLUTTERING

Clutter is a symbol of being held back. There may be important reasons for seeking protection from going forward in your life. However, sometimes when the reason for holding yourself back is no longer valid, you are still stuck with old decisions and old motivations.

If you suspect that you have stuff around you that is no longer a reflection of who you really are now, clear the air and let new energy into your life by uncluttering your space. You will be  astonished at the myriad positive effects that will emerge. First and foremost, you will attract a better flow of energy in your house and in your life. You will also notice a marked improvement in luck and prosperity for all the people who share the house with you.

The aim of uncluttering your space is to put every area of your life into perspective and balance. You will then be able to see clearly what you want, and you will have more time to do what you want. If you feel that you just don't know which path to follow in your life, clear the clutter from your home and you will find, even as you are clearing the junk, that ideas and thoughts of new directions come to you.

You will also find that the skills you gain as you clear the accumulated clutter of the past will help you to keep your life simple and organized. You will be able to find things much more quickly. You will also find that you can manage the flow of daily clutter easily, and that your workload will seem less overwhelming.

Once being organized becomes second nature to you, you will see more opportunities for advancement and will be in an excellent position to capitalize on them.

CLUTTER LOCATION CHECKLIST

Clutter can build up in a number of key areas. Go to each of the places identified in the checklist below and answer the questions before taking action to clear the clutter. The checklist is designed to help you clear the clutter and then keep it away permanently. The questions will help you identify where clutter has accumulated and help you notice any features that have created poison arrows aimed at the area in question; if there are, they may be the reason the clutter has built up over time.

LOCATION	Is there a lot of clutter in this area?	Is there a poison arrow aimed at this location?
Entrance to the home		
Hall table		
Bookcases		
Coffee table		
Kitchen table		
Kitchen countertops		
Kitchen cupboards		
Kitchen drawers		
Bedroom floors		
Bedroom closet		
Storage space in the cellar		
Storage space under the stairs		
Ironing board		
Kitchen cupboards		
Attic		
Garage		
Your car		
Shed		
Garden		
Study or computer room		
Filing cabinet		
Desk or workbench top		
Desk drawers		
Hidden areas at your place of work		
Workplace storage cupboards or bookshelves		
Outside storage facilities		
Homes of your friends or relatives		

KNOWING WHEN TO UNCLUTTER
AND SETTING UP THE BASICS

When you are ready to start the uncluttering process, you will need to set up a temporary area inside or outside your home or workplace. This is the area where you can immediately place the unwanted objects until you are ready to take them to the dump, donate them to charity, or give them away.

Setting up this area allows you to get the trash out of your selected space immediately. You may decide to have a temporary uncluttering storage area in the garage, in a prefabricated work shed bought specially for the job, or in the areas of your space that correspond with the health or family aspirations (see pages 18–21).

This area should be kept neat and clean while you sort through and figure out what to do with your clutter. If you do not keep this uncluttering space well organized, you may precipitate health problems for yourself.

To organize your temporary uncluttering storage area, consider setting up several large bins or bags for different types of clutter. Have bins or bags set up for each of the following categories:

- Keeping but needs to go in another area
- Unsure about throwing away
- Donating to a charitable organization
- Recycling cans, bottles, and newspapers
- Throwing away outright

Those objects you have chosen to keep from the area you are currently uncluttering can simply be left where they are. Clean them with a damp cloth or polish their surface, and clean each surface that you have uncluttered.

If you have a pair of Tibetan bells or a melodic bell, ring the bell over the surface you have uncluttered. At the end of a day's worth of

uncluttering or a discrete period of uncluttering, ring the bell over the temporary uncluttering storage area to help keep the energy flowing through that space.

Place a mirror on the door or entrance leading to the temporary uncluttering storage area. In feng shui, the mirror creates an illusion that the room does not exist.

So that you do not leave the clutter in your temporary setup, hang wind chimes or a natural crystal over the bins or bags. At the end of the day, go through your "unsure" pile and ask yourself the following questions:

- Am I going to use this item?
- What is this item for?
- Is this item a "want" or a "need?"
- Will I be seriously inconvenienced if I throw this item away?

If you still feel doubtful about whether or not you should discard the item, just bite the bullet and throw or give it away. That you are doubtful is a sure sign that you don't really need the object.

FENG SHUI TIP

Paul, a successful plumber, was asked by a friend to fix a dishwasher. Paul had a look at it and, after dismantling it, found that the dishwasher just could not be repaired. He then left the broken machine sitting beside the front door to his business. The broken dishwasher stayed there for quite a while. Soon Paul found that his business had slowed down, for no perceivable reason—he had always had a steady and reliable clientele—and that he was owed money. When his friend called to find out how the repairs were coming along, Paul finally asked him to take the machine away. With the machine gone, Paul was delighted to find that virtually the next day the money that was owed to him came in the mail. His business grew back to where it had been before the dishwasher arrived on his premises.

MANAGING LONG-TERM CLUTTER

Storing an object that you will use in the future is valid. However, you must be able to identify when in the future you will use the item and how often. If any question mark about its use lingers, it is best to get rid of it.

If you have hardware items (such as a power saw), remember that you are responsible for keeping them in good condition. You must be able to store them properly so that they don't get damaged and will stay in good working order.

Storage of other items, such as nails or paint, must also be carefully planned—nails will rust if they are incorrectly stored, and paint will crust over and become unusable.

Remember, if you choose to store something, you are responsible for its proper maintenance. It's important that the future use of your belongings will not be undermined by poor maintenance and storage, and that they will not quickly become useless pieces of junk. Also make sure that you know for what purpose an item will be used. If you don't know what it is, get rid of it. How many of us

---

FENG SHUI TIP

If you have difficulty discarding some items, consider packing them in a box and placing them neatly in a storage area. Make a note in your diary or special Uncluttering Journal (see opposite) to check in twelve months whether you have needed the things in the box. If you haven't missed them for twelve months, it is time to let them go.

---

have extension cords that have been gathering dust for years in a cupboard somewhere?

Also ask yourself whether you actually need the item or whether you only want it. If you are definitely going to use the object, then you need it and must find a suitable place to store it and look after it. If you just simply like the look of the object, or it was on sale and you couldn't resist buying it, then you wanted to acquire the object to fulfill an emotional need. However, buying an object is often not enough to actually quench your need to show how clever you were to find something that is both beautiful and cheap, or to remind you of a time or place when you were much happier.

STARTING AN UNCLUTTERING JOURNAL

When you are serious about uncluttering your space, an "Uncluttering Journal" is an absolute must. It will help you to keep track of the stage your uncluttering has reached. This is especially helpful if you have a family or staff team working with you on the uncluttering process.

The journal can house a multitude of information and ideas. You do not have to use a "day-by-day" planner; any lined journal will do. Choose a book that has good-quality paper, as you may want to paste in lists and photographs, as well as write down your impressions of how the project is going and jot down ideas from friends and books (such as this one) that you can implement.

The journal also acts as a symbol of what you are trying to do in your life—simplify and consolidate your lifestyle or business practices. By placing the information on this important topic in one easily accessible book, you are creating a focus for the project and adding depth to the process.

Keep a pen near the journal so that any idea can be quickly written down. If you are using a spiral-bound book, keep a pen inside the spirals so that it is always handy.

SIMPLE TIME-MANAGEMENT IDEAS

When contemplating removing long-term clutter, remember that it will take a while for you to clear your space. After all, it may have taken you a lifetime to accumulate the clutter! Making your uncluttering jobs small—doable in an evening or in even smaller time periods, such as fifteen minutes or half an hour—will help to simplify your life. The jobs can even become fun.

A step-by-step approach to uncluttering can help you get in touch with your past and may help you resolve issues that you have not had the time or the energy to examine. The process can also help you get in touch with your likes and dislikes. Uncluttering can help you free yourself from items that others have wanted you to have and expectations that have been placed on you by others.

However, it is important to keep an agenda or list of what needs to be uncluttered so that you do not fall behind in your plan to unclutter your home or workplace. Give yourself deadlines so that you can finish one task on your list or agenda per day or per week.

If you are doing your uncluttering once a week, make it the same day and time each week, so that you develop a routine of uncluttering. Similarly, if you are doing your uncluttering daily, choose the same time slot each day. By choosing the same time or day, you are training your mind to incorporate this activity into your daily routine, which may also stabilize the rest of your existing routine.

If your uncluttering task does not take up the full half hour, do not start on another task. Leave it for the next day or the next week. It is important not to discourage yourself by attempting to tackle too big a job.

When choosing the time for daily uncluttering, select a time when you are still active from the day. As soon as you walk in the door of your home, take a moment to check your entrance hall.

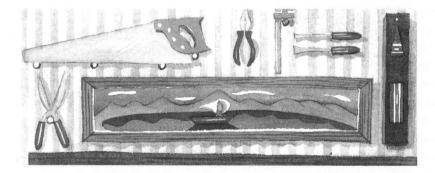

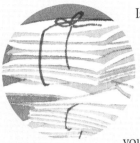

Is it warm and inviting? Is it clear of clothes and paper? Is there a space where you can put the junk mail and letters that are in your hand?

When considering implementing an uncluttering system, take into account how you interact with your space. Be aware about what you do as soon as you enter your home after a day at work or enter your workplace first thing in the morning. What is your first action? Do you bring in the mail? Is there a stack of newspapers at the entrance to your space? What do you do with the newspapers? What do you do with the mail and junk mail?

The first step is to prevent all unnecessary daily clutter from even coming into your home. Near the mailbox, have an all-weather paper recycling box large enough to hold any junk mail that still comes through. Unless it is pouring rain and you have no shelter, take the time each day to open your mail and pop any unnecessary information and torn envelopes into the recycling box before you even enter the house.

Once you bring the mail into your home, immediately file it in a series of shallow boxes or trays in the kitchen or family room. Have categories written prominently on the boxes, such as "bills," "school information," "bank statements," or "coupons."

If you are bringing in the shopping, have a box set aside in or near the kitchen for any plastic or paper bags that you bring into the house. Keep these bags to a minimum by taking your own shopping bag with you, asking for less packaging, recycling the bags, or returning the bags to retailers who recycle.

SPRING CLEANING

Spring is one of the traditional times for renewing your energies and those of your home. The increase in the sun's energy at this time of year is reflected in a feeling of increased creativity and an interest in exploring new activities. By removing clutter and the stale energy of winter from the house, you are creating space for a new energy to come in and revitalize you and your family. Doing so will make you feel linked with the energies of the season.

If you are using feng shui principles, you do not have to wait until spring to clean your space. In the *Tong Shu,* the feng shui almanac of lucky and unlucky days, there are specific days designated for housecleaning, usually spaced two weeks apart. If

you don't have access to the *Tong Shu,* consider, as a general rule, dusting and removing clutter from your space on a day that suits you once every two weeks.

If you are feeling unfocused, aimless, or in a rut, consider removing clutter from your premises. Often the amassing of a lot of material objects is an indication of stagnation. This stagnation may be a sign that you are unhappy with your life and that you are using the clutter around you as a barricade.

It is probably unreasonable to expect to clear all your clutter in one day, unless you really wish to make a fresh start, getting rid of everything at once. This approach can have advantages, but it will not give you the insight into your life that consciously and carefully uncluttering your space can give you.

You may find that the whole concept of uncluttering your space is just too daunting. If you do, do not despair. Uncluttering doesn't have to be an arduous chore. You can unclutter in small chunks, working on one small group of your possessions at a time, such as your accessories or the sock drawer.

If you don't know where to start to unclutter your space, stand at your front door and look at the interior of your house. Can you see a clutter of books, papers, furniture, or objects from the front door? This is the first area you will need to tidy up, because it is the first obstacle placed in the path of the qi energy's movement through your house. Alternatively, you could begin by neatening the area that corresponds to a problem in your life (see pages 18–21).

Clearing clutter takes time. You will need to sort through what has been accumulated and figure out whether you want to keep it or discard it. If you do need to keep some of your things, consider whether storage will be a problem. If you have no time to clear the space but would like to start the clearing process, try placing or hanging a clear quartz crystal on the pile of clutter. Wash the crystal in some running water before positioning it. The crystal will attract positive energy to the space, and will also encourage you to come into it to start clearing up.

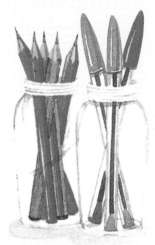

FENG SHUI TIP

Here are some quick uncluttering questions and answers:
- Can you see a poison arrow aimed at the area that is accumulating clutter (see pages 26–27)? If you can, consider blocking the feature creating the poison arrow by using a mirror, plant, crystal, or wind chime.
- Are you living or working in a safe neighborhood? If you are not, consider installing an effective security system.
- Do you feel emotionally vulnerable? If you do, consider talking about your feelings to a friend or a counselor. Uncluttering will help you to clear old patterns of behavior and look at problems and difficult issues in a different way.

WATER AND WATER FEATURES

According to feng shui principles, a water feature
must be incorporated in the garden to encourage the
flow of beneficial energy. A water feature can be used
to maximum benefit in a number of different
aspirations: the area that corresponds to wealth (southeast), the area
that corresponds to family and health (east), and the area that
corresponds to career (north).

The water feature can be anything from a birdbath to an
elaborate waterfall or a wall fountain. It must be rounded in shape,
preferably either circular or kidney-shaped. It is important that the
pool looks as natural as possible. There are many ornate fountains
that can be incorporated into a formal garden. However, in feng
shui, the emphasis is on moving away from traditional formal
garden designs that use symmetrical square or rectangular garden
beds and toward landscaped gardens that echo the flow of the yin
and yang symbol.

A water feature is another way to introduce the feng shui
remedies of sound (see page 159), especially if the water feature is
constructed so that water falls from a height, and movement (see
page 129). The sound of falling water is relaxing, and is an excellent,
gentle way to stimulate qi in a house, garden, or workplace.

Although water is a gentle cure, it is also an extremely powerful
one. In an area that has too much yang energy, install a small
waterfall or other water feature that allows water to fall and be
recycled; such a water feature would benefit an area in the garden
where the garden beds are drying out or an area where a straight
path ends.

Install a circular water feature in an area where the paths and
divisions of the garden create a rectangular pattern full of straight
lines. The nurturing energy of this feng shui cure will nourish these
areas and bring yin energy into the garden to help evoke a soothing,
calming atmosphere. Pools should be slightly curved or kidney

shaped rather than straight edged, and the curves should appear to "hug" the building. It is important to keep the water moving—it should not be allowed to become stagnant.

Water features are excellent ways of "curing" or dissipating negative energy, which can be created in a number of ways—by a poison arrow (created by poles and other sharp-angled features of the environment outside your building), an unpleasant view in the immediate vicinity, or the unchecked flow of the usually disruptive energy from the west.

If your house or business is situated at a T-intersection, you can stop the force of the poison arrow aimed at your front door or reception area by placing an attractively landscaped pool in the front yard or in front of the reception area. Ideally, the water feature should be installed at a minimum distance of ten feet from your front entrance.

If you have a swimming pool in your backyard, an area that is already yin in energy, you run the risk of creating an overly yin energy in this private area. The solution is to incorporate more yang energy objects—a garden structure such as an attractive bathhouse or pergola, perhaps, which you can use as a changing room or a place to rest in after a swim. If you are installing a swimming pool, make sure the design is in proportion to the house and property.

It is important to keep all water features in the garden in good repair and not to allow stagnation to creep in. It is believed that water draining or dripping away, especially into the earth, evokes a destructive energy between the elements, which then becomes an unlucky or inauspicious flow of energy in your garden and your life. In feng shui, it is believed that such leaks and disrepair will be reflected in financial problems, particularly the feeling that your money seems to just disappear.

WEALTH ASPIRATION

To enhance the flow of beneficial qi in the area of your house or place of business that resonates with wealth qi, you will first need to identify your wealth area (see pages 18–21) and then use auspicious symbols to attract wealth and good luck into your life.

According to the ancient Chinese beliefs system, there are three types of luck. As well as fate and the luck that you create for yourself, there is also a form of luck that encompasses feng shui, called "Earth Luck." This type of luck is created when you are attuned with the energy of the earth using feng shui principles, and it helps you to mitigate even the worst of fates.

The placement of good luck or wealth symbols in the home is important. Never place them on the floor or in a low position. These symbols need to be placed in an elevated location, such as on a mantelpiece or above the door.

When decorating your wealth area, keep in mind that this area resonates with the element of wood, and allow this to influence the color schemes and objects you use to decorate this part of the house. Light greens and shades of brown and tan will enhance the wealth energy in your home, as will incorporating potted plants. One simple way to increase your wealth is to place three gold-colored coins that have been wrapped in red paper under a potted plant.

Metal is harmful to Wood, so do not use much metal; concentrate on Water and Wood motifs. You may even consider installing an

---

FENG SHUI TIP

Here are some Chinese good luck numbers:

2 – Easy fulfillment   **5** – Good luck

6 – Wealth   **8** – Good business, wealth

9 – Recognition, completion   **10** – Confidence

aquarium with nine fish, preferably eight goldfish and one black fish (see page 88). The symbolic role of the black fish is to attract and destroy bad wealth energy that strays into your home.

If you are building a new house or repaving your driveway, consider burying six coins in your driveway before you lay the cement, gravel, or paving stones. Bury the coins along an imaginary line that leads to your entrance, as this will attract abundant wealth energy to your door. Alternatively, place nine coins under your welcome mat.

In feng shui, certain numbers attract good or bad luck. For example, the number four is believed to be bad luck, auguring death, while five is thought to be a lucky number because it symbolizes the five elements—Earth, Water, Fire, Wood, and Metal—that form the basis of Chinese medicine and religious beliefs.

We all have lucky numbers, which are worked out according to the formulas outlined on pages 58–59. Using the luo-shu square, you can use your lucky numbers to work out which areas are favorable to you (see pages 122–123). However, what if the area that corresponds with the wealth qi is in a direction unfavorable to you? Work out your lucky number and the directions that are favorable to you. If the wealth area is not in a favorable direction, you can balance the wealth area in your favor. This can be done by placing a bowl of water in the wealth area. Remember to change the water every few days.

If your house or place of business is an irregular shape and the particular corner that resonates with wealth qi is missing, you will continually have problems with your finances. The cure is to square off that portion of the building and make it appear to be a regular shape. To square off, continue the lines of the two walls that would make up that corner and find the point in the garden where they meet. To emphasize this projected corner, feng shui practitioners often advise including a water fountain or other water feature.

To enhance the wealth aspiration, you may wish to make a kidney-shaped pond and have a few goldfish or, if there is enough room, some carp, swimming in it.

If your wealth corner contains one of the house's water features, such as a bathroom, toilet, kitchen, or laundry, be careful that you are not flushing away your wealth energy.

Wealth is particularly linked with yin energy and the element of Water. It follows that all areas in your home dealing with water, such as sinks, bathtubs, laundry tubs, and toilets, must be in good working order and not blocked in any way.

So that you are not losing your wealth, it is important to do the following things:

- Fix leaky taps immediately.
- Always flush your toilet with the lid down.
- Cover all floor drain holes and sink holes.
- Keep the laundry, toilet, and bathroom doors closed at all times.

In feng shui, a number of symbols can be used in either your home or your business to stimulate success in your life. An extensive range of symbols or "lucky objects" has developed in China over the centuries.

These symbols include objects such as coins, statues, vases, and fans that are believed to attract beneficial energy or disperse negative energy. You can use the symbols in one of two ways.

The first technique requires you to clear the energy of the space at the point where you wish the symbol to be placed, or where you feel instinctively it should be placed. Clear all the clutter and clean or dust the area to allow the symbol to work with an unimpeded flow of energy. If you want to be more specific, place a chosen symbol in a particular aspiration area of your home, business, bedroom, or desk.

With the second method, hang or place the symbol above clutter in your wealth sector and let it help to clear the energy around the clutter. If you use the symbol in this way, you will be amazed at how you will soon become inspired to clear the clutter.

FENG SHUI TIP

Plant some golden clumping bamboo in the backyard to help nurture your financial prospects.

Symbols used to attract finance to an individual or a business should always be placed at or above eye level. The color of wealth symbols should be either gold or bright yellow. These colors are yang, or aggressive in energy, and should be used sparingly, as a highlight in your interior decoration. The colors can occur either naturally, as in a goldfish or a piece of yellow fruit, or as a gilded or bronze metal coin.

Although the element of Metal is destructive to Wood, the element that resonates to the wealth aspiration, metal coins can be used sparingly to enhance financial success, particularly if a red tassel is hung from the coin or series of coins or if the coins are wrapped in red paper. It is believed that the color red enhances the strength of the wealth symbol. Multiple-coin charms are always tied together with red thread.

In feng shui, prosperity charms abound. They usually combine a number of images that are thought to attract wealth and abundance. The images include special Chinese words and charms, three-dimensional miniature versions of animals thought to be lucky, such as fish, bats, and stags, and coins, bells, and tassels. The charms can be made from a wide variety of materials, ranging from plastic to gold and jade.

WIND CHIMES

A FENG SHUI CURE

Wind chimes and bells help to activate stagnant energy in a building. Corners are particularly notorious for the buildup of stagnant negative energy. Wind chimes are also excellent for slowing down energy that is rushing along a straight corridor or flight of stairs. If the front door is positioned in view of the back door, this encourages the fast passage of qi energy through the house, and does not allow the energy to move beneficially throughout the building.

Wind chimes placed near the front door will help to slow down the energy, encouraging it to move into different areas of the house rather than out the back door. For the interior of a building, use only hollow metal or bamboo wind chimes, preferably with five or six tubes.

Solid metal wind chimes can be hung outside your front door to attract positive energy to you, especially if your front door faces west or north. Do not use this cure if your entrance faces east—this compass direction corresponds to the element of Wood, which is capable of being "destroyed" by Metal.

Choose wind chimes that sound melodious to your ears, as chimes, whether they are made of metal, wood, or bamboo, can attract prosperous energy into the building. The sound of moving water also enhances beneficial energy.

If you sit under a beam, either move, or hang a wind chime directly overhead to dissipate the negative, oppressive energy that the beam is directing toward you. Also, consider hanging a wind chime in front of a protruding corner to dissipate the poison arrows created in that area.

Wind chimes can also be used to stimulate and improve the flow of energy in the northwest section of the building, which corresponds to the mentors and travel aspiration (see pages 18–21).

WINDOW BOXES

Window boxes are a delightful way of screening an unpleasant view and generating a flow of positive energy into your home. Both balconies and window boxes, no matter which area they are in, can enhance the flow of energy through a particular aspiration area (see pages 14–15).

It is important that the plants used in the window box are compatible, nurturing each other's growth, and that the window boxes are positioned in windows that are not exposed to strong winds and harsh, sunny conditions. Always keep an eye on your window boxes—water them on a regular basis, as they are more likely to dry out.

Attractive, flowering plants that could be used for sunny window boxes include white, pink, or scarlet nicotianas, blue or purple salvias, and miniature roses. Many of these grow upright and will cover the lower half of a window with pretty flowers. For shady window boxes, try ferns, hostas, and other moisture-loving plants.

In some feng shui schools, it is believed that the best type of window for the auspicious circulation of beneficial energy is the sort that opens outward. Outward-opening windows tend to preclude a window box unless the top of the box is below the windowsill; the window box should also contain plants that cascade over it in rounded shapes, such as fuchsias, or that spread and spill over the edge of the window box, such as yellow or white zinnias and lobelia.

FENG SHUI TIP

When figuring out what to plant in your window boxes, keep in mind the need to have a balance between rounded (yin) and elongated (yang) leaf shapes and to include some vibrant colors in the arrangement to stimulate the flow of beneficial energy.

WINDOWS

SEE ALSO **CURTAINS** ON PAGE 67.

Open windows let beneficial qi enter into a home or workplace, allowing both fresh air and energy to flow through stagnant areas. When the sun is shining, a window will let in beneficial yang energy, alleviating the most depressed mood. Yang energy is also generated by pleasant views seen through a particular window. However, if it is too hot and dry, the window will allow an overly yang energy to enter into the house, which can generate a sense of disharmony.

However, when the sun is not shining and the weather is stormy or misty, the same window can generate yin energy that can oppress the energy of a room and its occupants, particularly if the room is already decorated with dark-colored fabric, wallpaper, and furniture.

As the window reflects the mood of the weather and the seasons, it is good feng shui to have a window covering installed so that you

---

FENG SHUI TIP

If there is an unpleasant view from one of the windows of your house, consider replanting your garden in that particular direction to include protective planting and screening. This will benefit the flow of energy not only to the house but also in the garden. Many different types of shrubs can be successfully turned into protective plantings. Those that have, in certain seasons, a scent, bright flowers, or brightly colored leaves are favored in feng shui gardening, as these attract positive energy, and this energy will flow from your garden into your home. Prune your hedge into a formal, rounded shape or plant an informal hedge instead. Also consider including in your hedge a round-leafed plant such as the firethorn (*Pyracantha* species). Other suggestions include:
- Scented hedges—orange jasmine (*Murraya paniculata*)
- Brightly flowered hedges—camellias (such as *Camellia sasanqua*)
- Hedges with brightly colored leaves—photinia (such as *Photinia* 'Rubens')

can regulate how much yang or yin energy you would like to let
into your interior, allowing you to assess whether the energy
outside is beneficial to your particular room.

It is bad feng shui to have a window completely uncovered.
Keeping the window curtains open during the evening is also
considered bad feng shui. This is because the yin energy of night
will overwhelm the yang energy emanating from the lights in the
house or workplace. This will substantially affect your energy levels
in the evening. Unless you wish to sleep and rise with the sun,
install window coverings as a priority.

When measuring for your window coverings, take the
opportunity to check that your window measurements are
auspicious—see page 87. If your window measurements are
inauspicious, you can install curtains or blinds of an auspicious
size to mask your window.

It is important that the windows of a room are well
proportioned and that they are not overly large or too small. If they
are very large, make sure that you install a curtain or some other
window covering. If they are too small and the room is still dark,
consider installing another window. If you are not able to install
another window, consider increasing the number of lamps or the
wattage of lightbulbs used in this room.

A poison arrow seen through a window can affect your interior
and you may find that clutter always accumulates in the affected
area. Either install a window box with enough plants to shield
your interior from the poison arrow or place a potted plant or silk
flowers on the sill. Consider also hanging a crystal from the
window frame to disperse negative energy from the poison arrow
or an unpleasant view.

WORK STRESS

In feng shui, your career aspiration corresponds to the north section of your home or office and to the area directly in front of you as you sit at your desk. Stress can occur at work for many reasons and these fall into one of two broad categories—yang-related and yin-related stress.

Yang-related stress arises from overstimulation of this energy. It can lead to impulsive resignations, argumentativeness, overwork, and high absenteeism. This form of stress is prevalent in jobs where a person is required to work all day in front of a computer. As the career section of your desk corresponds to the space immediately in front of you when you are sitting down, positioning your computer in this area may lead to your feeling overworked and tired. This is because computers continually generate a stimulating form of yang energy.

To counter this form of stress, place a yin feature on the right-hand side of the computer, as the right-hand side corresponds to yang energy. Balancing the yin and yang in this area will help to rebalance your feelings about your work, and will lead to rebalancing your workload.

If you are constantly using your hands and like to wear jewelry, consider wearing a hematite or lapis lazuli ring or bracelet. Hematite is a semiprecious stone that is used by feng shui practitioners for a variety of cures, including the relief of stress.

Yin-related stress occurs when there is a feeling of stagnation

---

FENG SHUI TIP

It is important that low morale is countered by the incorporation of yang features in your building's interior. This will increase feelings of expansiveness among the staff. Incorporate upward-facing lamps, large paintings, posters, and generously proportioned furniture in the workplace, and remove any broken furniture and out-of-date machinery.

about your work. This can have a number of reasons—lack of confidence that you can get the job you want, or feelings of not being valued for what you can really do, for instance. This kind of stress leads to apathy, long-drawn-out plans to resign, lack of focus, and poor job performance.

To stimulate the acknowledgment aspiration in feng shui, focus on the southern area of your home and your workplace. On your desk, this area is directly opposite where you sit, near the top of your table or desk. Clear this space and counter any poison arrows aimed at this particular area (see pages 26–27).

When you have cleared this area, place a light there that you can keep lit for at least a couple of hours a day. If you work with your back to the door, you may find that your stress levels are heightened. You can cure this by either repositioning your desk so that you can see the entrance or by placing a small mirror in the acknowledgment area so that you can see the entrance while you work. This will not only stimulate positive energy for this aspiration, but also alleviate the stress caused by not facing your entrance.

Carry a piece of white jade to work to attract good luck—jade is an excellent healing stone. You may also consider wearing or carrying some lapis lazuli—this will help to alleviate feelings of depression.

FENG SHUI TIP

If you are suffering from a stress-related illness, place an open fan in the career section of your home, master bedroom, workplace, or corresponding area on your desk (see pages 18–19). If you are artistic, you may wish to paint, draw, or even paste an image of a horse (for endurance) or a monkey (for health and protection) on the fan and hang a green tassel, symbolizing health, from one end. To balance the flow of yin/yang energy by your bed, place two small brass figurines of goats or horses on either side of the bed, perhaps on your side tables, on the top of the headboard on each side, or on a shelf above your head.

WORKPLACE LOCATION

Traditionally, it was believed that living and working in an area where the streets all run parallel to each other in a grid formation caused bad feng shui, but now only busy thoroughfares are believed to be bad feng shui. Even the fast-flowing energy of these thoroughfares can be remedied to a certain extent by planting trees along the sides of the street.

Buildings in general have a predominantly yang energy. The bigger your workplace, the more important is it to balance the forcefulness of yang energy with softer yin energy. Yin energy is contained in the landscaping around the building. It is most auspicious to have a park near a large building, preferably with a fountain or other water feature in the middle.

It is prudent to avoid working near areas or in buildings that have a poor balance of yin and yang energy. Buildings correspond with yang energy and landscaping corresponds with yin energy. Look at whether the building and the landscaping are in balance with each other. Also look at the design of the building and its neighbors—do they have sharp or precipitous design features, like a steep roofline or downward-pointing arrows? If so, you may find that the tenants or owners of the buildings are suffering from declines in profit, poor business, and low morale.

FENG SHUI TIP

Try the following solutions:
- If you work near a railway, place a large earthenware pot outside your main entrance.
- If you work near an airport, incorporate a large, external sculpture to hold down the energy or use big, heavy paperweights when you are working.
- If you work near a police station, use peach colors with a little yellow in the decor of your business.
- If you work near sewage plants or garbage dumps, plant trees and bright, fragrant flowers near your main entrance.
- If you work near an undertaker, place a water feature outside your main entrance.

Workplaces such as schools, stock exchanges, and buildings with a lot of machinery contain a lot of yang energy. These environments can cause people working there to feel a constant, low-level anxiety unless there is a good counterbalance of yin energy, such as potted plants and the use of dark colors or dark woods for wall paneling or furniture.

If you do work in such an environment, take care to spend weekends and holidays in the country or on the water, to help revive your energy. There is an old feng shui saying that if you have bad luck, you should travel over water to wash it away.

Places that are excessively yin in energy are frequently associated with death, grieving, and other feelings of distress. It is best to avoid working near churches, graveyards, and police stations. Working near sewage plants and garbage dumps also encourages negative energy to enter your workplace.

When setting up or relocating your business, take into consideration various feng shui principles. First, be sure to find out what happened to the previous owners of the premises. If they relocated because they were expanding or the owners retired after a long and successful work life, the premises are more than likely to be auspicious. If the previous owners or tenants went bankrupt, suffered from embezzlement,  low morale, or high turnover of staff, or failed to pay their rent or mortgage on time, it is best to avoid these premises.

It is considered most auspicious to open your business after the new moon. In the Chinese calendar, each day is categorized as lucky or unlucky. To find out whether the day your business started was lucky or to schedule a date for the start of your business, an English version of an important Chinese almanac, the *Tong Shu,* is available every year. This almanac also lists lucky and unlucky times of the day.

CHINESE CHART OF YEARS

NEW YEAR DATE	ELEMENT	YIN/YANG	FEMALE (East/West)	MALE (East/West)
1919 Feb 1	Earth	Yin	West	East
1920 Feb 20	Metal	Yang	West	West
1921 Feb 8	Metal	Yin	West	West
1922 Jan 28	Water	Yang	East	West
1923 Feb 16	Water	Yin	East	West
1924 Feb 5	Wood	Yang	West	East
1925 Jan 24	Wood	Yin	East	East
1926 Feb 13	Fire	Yang	East	West
1927 Feb 2	Fire	Yin	West	East
1928 Jan 23	Earth	Yang	West	East
1929 Feb 10	Earth	Yin	West	West
1930 Jan 30	Metal	Yang	West	West
1931 Feb 17	Metal	Yin	East	West
1932 Feb 6	Water	Yang	East	West
1933 Jan 26	Water	Yin	West	East
1934 Feb 14	Wood	Yang	East	East
1935 Feb 4	Wood	Yin	East	West
1936 Jan 31	Fire	Yang	West	East
1937 Feb 11	Fire	Yin	West	East
1938 Jan 31	Earth	Yang	West	West
1939 Feb 19	Earth	Yin	West	West
1940 Feb 8	Metal	Yang	East	West
1941 Jan 27	Metal	Yin	East	West
1942 Feb 18	Water	Yang	West	East
1943 Feb 5	Water	Yin	East	East
1944 Jan 25	Wood	Yang	East	West
1945 Feb 13	Wood	Yin	West	East
1946 Feb 2	Fire	Yang	West	East
1947 Jan 22	Fire	Yin	West	West
1948 Feb 10	Earth	Yang	West	West
1949 Jan 29	Earth	Yin	East	West
1950 Feb 17	Metal	Yang	East	West
1951 Feb 6	Metal	Yin	West	East
1952 Jan 27	Water	Yang	East	East
1953 Feb 14	Water	Yin	East	West
1954 Feb 3	Wood	Yang	West	East
1955 Jan 24	Wood	Yin	West	East
1956 Feb 12	Fire	Yang	West	West
1957 Jan 31	Fire	Yin	West	West
1958 Feb 18	Earth	Yang	East	West
1959 Feb 8	Earth	Yin	East	West
1960 Jan 28	Metal	Yang	West	East

NEW YEAR DATE	ELEMENT	YIN/YANG	FEMALE (East/West)	MALE (East/West)
1961 Feb 15	Metal	Yin	East	East
1962 Feb 5	Water	Yang	East	West
1963 Jan 25	Water	Yin	West	East
1964 Feb 13	Wood	Yang	West	East
1965 Feb 2	Wood	Yin	West	West
1966 Jan 21	Fire	Yang	West	West
1967 Feb 9	Fire	Yin	East	West
1968 Jan 30	Earth	Yang	East	West
1969 Feb 17	Earth	Yin	West	East
1970 Feb 6	Metal	Yang	East	East
1971 Jan 27	Metal	Yin	East	West
1972 Feb 15	Water	Yang	West	East
1973 Feb 3	Water	Yin	West	East
1974 Jan 23	Wood	Yang	West	West
1975 Feb 11	Wood	Yin	West	West
1976 Jan 31	Fire	Yang	East	West
1977 Feb 18	Fire	Yin	East	West
1978 Feb 7	Earth	Yang	West	East
1979 Jan 28	Earth	Yin	East	East
1980 Feb 16	Metal	Yang	East	West
1981 Feb 5	Metal	Yin	West	East
1982 Jan 25	Water	Yang	West	East
1983 Feb 13	Water	Yin	West	West
1984 Feb 2	Wood	Yang	West	West
1985 Feb 20	Wood	Yin	East	West
1986 Feb 9	Fire	Yang	East	West
1987 Jan 29	Fire	Yin	West	East
1988 Feb 17	Earth	Yang	East	East
1989 Feb 6	Earth	Yin	East	West
1990 Jan 27	Metal	Yang	West	East
1991 Feb 15	Metal	Yin	West	East
1992 Feb 4	Water	Yang	West	West
1993 Jan 23	Water	Yin	West	West
1994 Feb 10	Wood	Yang	East	West
1995 Jan 31	Wood	Yin	East	West
1996 Feb 19	Fire	Yang	West	East
1997 Feb 7	Fire	Yin	East	East
1998 Jan 28	Earth	Yang	East	West
1999 Feb 16	Earth	Yin	West	East
2000 Feb 5	Metal	Yang	West	East
2001 Jan 24	Metal	Yin	West	West
2002 Feb 12	Water	Yang	West	West
2003 Feb 1	Water	Yin	East	West
2004 Jan 22	Wood	Yang	East	West
2005 Feb 9	Wood	Yin	West	East
2006 Jan 29	Fire	Yang	East	East
2007 Feb 18	Fire	Yin	East	West
2008 Feb 7	Earth	Yang	West	East

GLOSSARY

BAGUA Also known as pa-kwa. An octagonal image that contains trigrams representing the eight compass directions and corresponding aspirations, family members, numbers, and other feng shui correspondences, including yin and yang energy.

CELESTIAL ANIMALS Each cardinal point of the compass corresponds to a particular type of energy that is symbolized by one of four Celestial creatures. A southerly, lucky energy is represented as the Celestial Red Phoenix, while the Celestial Black Tortoise symbolizes a northerly, nurturing energy. The Celestial White Tiger symbolizes a westerly, unsettled energy and the Celestial Green Dragon symbolizes an easterly energy that represents knowledge and wisdom.

CURES There are two types of cures in feng shui. Renovation or some reconstruction of the environment to improve the flow of energy is a form of heavy-duty *rushi* cure, while *cushi* cures are symbolic objects or features, such as color, reflective surfaces, harmonious sounds, plants, pets, mobiles, flags, statues, rocks, fans, flutes, and electrical objects, that can simply be added to an environment to rebalance the flow of energy.

EIGHT ASPIRATIONS Also known as the eight enrichments, these are the aspects of life that include career, fame and acknowledgment, family and health, children and creativity, mentors and travel, knowledge and study, relationships, and wealth.

ELEMENTS There are five Chinese elements that affect the flow of qi in the environment. These are Earth, Wood, Fire, Metal, and Water. Each element resonates with a particular compass direction and with other aspects of life, including the eight aspirations. The art of feng shui includes identifying objects and directions that correspond to a particular element and balancing the elements to produce a productive flow of energy or rebalancing any elements placed in a destructive dynamic.

FENG SHUI Literally means (the flow of) wind and water. Feng shui is the art of manipulating an energy force called qi within the environment so that the energy flows in a gentle way without obstructions. When the energy is allowed to meander in a curved manner, good luck, prosperity, and success are attracted to the environment and to those who live in its vicinity.

MAGIC SQUARE Also known as luo-shu. A nine-grid square that can be used to identify where the eight aspirations fall in an interior or garden.

PA-KWA See Bagua.

POISON ARROWS Also known as secret arrows. A form of sha qi. They occur when a harmful shaft of energy is created by long, straight corridors, paths, or roads, or by sharp angles created by sloping rooflines and vertical objects such as telephone poles.

QI Also known as chi, this is an invisible life force that flows around everything. There are three interrelated types of qi—heaven qi, earth qi, and human qi. A beneficial flow of qi is called sheng qi, while a destructive flow of energy is known as sha qi.

SHA QI The negative form of energy that is either stagnant, like a blocked river or is made to move too quickly along long, straight corridors or streets. A poison arrow is a form of sha qi.

SHENG QI The beneficial flow of energy that moves through the environment gently, freely and without impediment, much like the flow of water in a slow, meandering river.

TRIGRAM A picture of three broken or unbroken lines stacked one upon the other. The broken lines correspond to yin energy while the unbroken lines correspond to yang energy. In a bagua there are eight three-line trigrams, which are positioned in a particular pattern around the edge of each side of the bagua.

YANG This type of energy corresponds to male, aggressive energy, bright colors, and the furniture and objects within an interior or garden.

YIN This type of energy corresponds to female, passive energy, dark colors, and the space within an interior or garden.

UNCLUTTERING A technique to help clear the surrounding environment to allow qi to move freely and without obstructions.

INDEX

acknowledgment aspiration, 14–19, 25, 30–31, 69, 181
advertisements, 37, 47
amenities, 32–33
animal pictures, 103
animal symbols, 34
arguments, 52–53
artwork, 35, 48, 50, 112, 180
aspirations, 14–17, 25, 54, 69, 186
   calculations, 18–21
attracting abundance, 36, 48, 70

bags, 144–145
   briefcase, 51, 114–115
bagua, 16–18, 22, 36, 108, 126, 186, 187
   deflective powers, 18, 27, 147
   template, 20–21
balconies, 63, 177
bamboo, 80, 144, 174
   flutes, 86
   wind chimes, 176
barbecue area, 76, 81
bathroom, 30, 32–33, 38–39, 140, 174
beams, 99, 151, 176
bedroom, 35, 40–41, 42, 73, 75, 102, 124, 140, 149–151, 161
bells, 42, 43, 53, 64, 73, 83, 90, 108–109, 150, 152, 159, 163, 175, 176
beneficial qi, 9, 31, 37, 47, 69, 82, 91, 97, 122, 126, 129, 134, 170, 178–179, 187
birds, 43, 141, 150, 151
birth
   animals, 34
   time, 134
   years, 34, 184–185
boardroom table, 125
bookcases, 93, 105
books, 44–45, 169
Buddha, 36, 98
business, 48–49, 129
   attracting customers, 37, 163
   expansion, 49
   improvement, 46, 126
   loan, 54
   logo, 7, 37, 47

name, 7, 47
opening day, 182
signs, 37, 47
business premises, 49, 108, 183
   location, 182–183
   office plan, 132–133
   office warming, 134–135
   orientation, 136, 137
   reception area, 146–147, 158
   uncluttering, 130–131
butterflies, 43, 112, 141

career, 6, 14–17, 50–51, 66, 69, 91, 114–115, 129, 180–181
celestial animals, 23, 98, 186
cell phone, 91
chair, 60, 70, 84, 92, 122, 125, 133, 158
chi energy, 6, 8
children, 14–16, 19, 25
   child's bedroom, 41, 73
   child's playhouse, 99
   electric blankets, 40
Chinese almanac, 134, 168, 182
Chinese astrological animals, 34
Chinese Chart of Years, 184–185
   application, 12
Chinese elements, 8, 12–13, 25, 54, 76–81, 142, 184–185, 186
   compatibility, 56–59
   incompatible energy chart, 12
Chinese good luck numbers, 172–173
chushi cures, 24, 186
cicadas, 103, 112
circle, 47
clocks, 40–41, 75, 105, 159
clothes, 156–157
clutter, 9, 15, 28, 38–39, 40, 51, 160–169
   aim of uncluttering, 160
   clothing, 156–157
   household, 106–107
   kitchen, 117, 161
   location checklist, 161
   office, 130–131

personal, 140, 161
strategies, 28–29, 44–45, 106–107, 156–157
time management ideas, 166–167
tips, 21, 29, 36, 42, 100, 106, 164, 169
uncluttering journal, 165
uncluttering process, 160, 162–169
work table, 68–69
coins, 36, 37, 43, 46, 48–49, 51, 54, 145, 152, 173–175
colors, 39, 40, 55, 67, 80, 89, 108, 113, 119, 126–127, 139, 141, 151, 172, 175, 177, 182
compass, 14, 16–18, 20–23
readings, 136, 137
compass school, 23
compatibility calculations, 56–59
computers, 68–69, 75, 130, 180
concentration, 60–61
Confucius, 118
courtyard, 31, 62
creativity, 14–19, 25, 64–65, 69
crystals, 26–27, 60, 66, 91, 105, 120, 129, 134, 148, 149, 163, 169
ball, 49
singing bowls, 159
cures, 15, 24–25, 34, 35, 42, 43, 52–55, 66–67, 88–89, 103, 113, 120, 124, 128–129, 152, 158, 159, 186
overuse, 118
curtains, 39, 67, 126–127, 179
cushions, 11, 51, 84, 89

desks, 30, 68–69, 104–105, 111, 121, 122, 132–133, 137, 161, 181
digital clock, 40–41, 75
dining room, 70–71
directions, 13, 17, 46, 54, 68, 82–83, 111, 114, 116, 118, 139, 142
east/west compatibility, 58–59, 111, 136–137
lucky, 122
doors, 71–72, 108, 111, 117, 174
dragon, 8, 31, 47, 98, 112, 115, 134
celestial green dragon, 23, 186
driveways, 139, 173

eagle, 43, 52, 115
earth element, 8, 12–13, 14, 17, 25, 41, 50, 54–57, 76–78, 126, 139, 142, 154, 186
new year dates, 184–185
earth luck, 172

earth qi, 8
education, 14–17, 74–75
electrical equipment, 75, 91, 159
elements, 8, 12–13, 25, 54, 76–81, 142, 184–185, 186
compatibility, 56–59
incompatible energy chart, 12
entrance, 31, 36, 43, 50, 72, 108, 111, 114, 128, 134–135, 137, 158
garden, 94–95
view from front door, 168–169

fame, 14, 16–19, 25, 30–31
family, 14–16, 82–83
family room, 84–85
fans, 86, 151, 174, 181
feng, 6, 187
feng shui, 187
art of placement, 6–7
beliefs, 6–7
intuition, 113
principles, 6–7
rules, 8–15
schools of thought, 9, 22–23
feng shui ruler, 72–73, 87, 93
fire, 37, 109, 134
fire element, 8, 12–13, 14, 25, 30–31, 33, 41, 54–59, 63, 76, 80–81, 116, 126, 139, 142, 154, 186
new year dates, 184–185
fireplace, 85
fish pond, 173
fish tanks, 36, 88
flags, 97, 129, 151
floor rugs, 89
flutes, 86, 151
form school, 23, 154–155
friendships, 90–91
mentor aspiration, 14–15, 17, 19, 69
frogs, 36, 48–49, 98
furniture, 71–73, 84, 87, 92–93, 95, 122, 125, 146, 148, 150, 158, 169, 178, 180–181

garden, 7, 11, 16, 20–21, 26–27, 30–31, 62–63, 65, 119, 161
elements, 76–81, 95, 97, 139, 142
furniture, 92, 95
lights, 96, 120–121
ornaments, 36, 97, 99, 112
paths, 76, 94–95, 138–139, 187
plantings, 76–81, 141–143, 144, 149, 178

statues, 98, 112, 127, 158
structures, 11, 79, 99, 112, 119, 138, 155
water feature, 78–79, 98, 170–171, 173, 182
geography, 23, 154–155, 182
gifts, 57, 100–101, 140

hardware items, 164
health, 14–19, 69, 102–103, 112, 181
heaven, 8, 47
heavy objects, 158
home, 7, 14, 20–23, 26–27, 66, 85, 108–109, 129, 153–155, 178–179, 181
choosing, 110–111
compatibility, 136–137
lucky areas, 122–123
spring cleaning, 168–169
home office, 104–105, 107, 137
honored guest, 84, 125
house materials, 155
house shapes, 155
household clutter, 106–107
housewarming, 108–109, 124
human qi, 8

I Ching, 22
imbalance, 10, 15
symptoms, 15
incense, 129, 148
insects, 112, 141
insomnia, 41
intuition, 113

jade Bi, 152
job interview, 51, 114–115

kitchen, 30, 32–33, 116–117, 174
knowledge, 14–15, 18–19, 25, 61, 69, 75, 99, 118–119
Kuan Yin, 91, 98

L-shaped area, 20, 26, 85, 155
landscape features, 23, 154–155, 182
lighting, 30–31, 37, 51, 54, 62–63, 66, 85, 91, 115, 120–121, 147, 180
garden, 96
Lin Hai, 46
living room, 84–85
longevity symbols, 103
love and romance, 86, 148–151
low productivity, 121, 180

luck, 43, 47, 49, 51, 52, 54, 134, 172
Chinese good luck numbers, 172–173
love symbols, 150–151
lucky areas, 122–123
lucky days, 29, 168, 183
lucky direction, 122
lucky objects, 174
luo-pan compass, 22, 69
luo-shu, 18, 22, 123, 173, 187

magazines, 44–45
magic square, 18–19, 22, 123, 173, 187
mentors, 14–15, 17, 19, 69, 90, 126–127
metal element, 8, 12–13, 14, 25, 50, 54–59, 64, 76, 78, 126, 139, 142, 154, 172, 173, 175, 176, 186
new year dates, 184–185
mirrors, 26–27, 31, 40, 43, 46, 48, 70, 83, 85, 91, 115, 117, 120–121, 124, 128, 147, 150, 163, 169, 181
movement, 129
music, 60–61, 75, 126, 135, 159

neighbor problems, 124–125
new year dates, 184–185

office clutter, 130–131
office equipment, 69, 180–181
office plan, 132–133
office warming, 134–135
orientation, 16–23, 58–59
building, 122–123, 136
template, 20–21

pagoda, 99, 119
paintings, 35, 48, 50, 53, 60, 148, 180
pa-kwa, 16–17
paths, 76, 94–95, 138–139, 187
pavement, 138–139, 173
personal clutter, 140, 161
personal qi, 9
pets, 141
pillows, 85
plants, 31, 55, 77–81, 94–95, 99, 141, 142–143, 144, 177
hedges, 77, 80, 142, 178
potted, 11, 36, 39, 77, 147, 169, 172, 179, 183
poison arrows, 7, 9, 18, 20, 26–29, 49, 51–53, 67, 70, 72, 86, 90, 93, 125, 133, 146–145, 149, 154, 169, 171, 179, 187

promotion, 6, 14–15, 50–51, 69
prosperity, 6, 14–15, 34, 36, 116, 144, 145
  charms, 36, 175
  purses, 144–145

qi energy, 6–10, 16, 24–25, 30–31, 35, 52, 72–73, 113, 158, 176, 187
  block, 7, 9, 25–26
  conductors, 23
  flow, 6–7, 9–11, 16

rectangles, 142, 155
recycling, 162, 167
relationships, 14–19, 25, 57, 69, 129, 140
  love and romance, 148–151
  making amends and keeping the peace, 124–125
retrenchment, 15, 69
ritual for removing negative energy, 152
roads, 18, 153, 184, 187
  T-intersection, 153, 171
roof line, 18, 53, 72, 99, 129
rushi cures, 24, 186

salt, 71
sculpture, 35, 64–65, 112
seasons, 13
secret arrows, 9
semiprecious stones, 61, 64, 66, 91, 180–11
sha qi, 9, 72, 187
shapes, 154–155, 182
sheng qi, 9, 187
shoes, 156–157
shui, 6, 187
sound, 60–61, 75, 91, 126, 135, 159, 170
spring cleaning, 168–169
square, 47, 142, 155
statues, 35, 65, 98, 127, 158, 174
stereo equipment, 75, 85, 90, 159
stove, 33, 116
street, 18, 153, 171, 184, 187
street numbers, 7
stress, 180–181
study, 14–15, 19, 60–61, 118–119
swimming pool, 78, 98, 171

table decoration, 71, 125
television, 40, 75, 85, 159
terraces, 62–63

time management ideas, 166–167
toilet, 30, 32–33, 39, 40, 46, 174
Tong Shu, 134, 168, 182
travel, 14–15, 18–19, 25, 69, 126–127, 134, 183
trees, 76, 79, 142–143, 149, 182
triangles, 37, 80, 142, 155
trigram, 17, 187
  example, 16

wallet, 144–145
water, 6, 46, 68, 187
water element, 8, 12–13, 14, 25, 33, 39, 50, 54–59, 76, 78–79, 116, 126, 139, 142, 144, 154, 172–174, 186
  new year dates, 184–185
water feature, 78–79, 98, 170–171, 173, 182
wealth, 14–19, 25, 30, 32, 36, 46, 66, 69, 141, 144, 172–175
  business, 48–49, 54
weather vanes, 97, 129
whirligigs, 129
wind, 6, 97, 129, 187
wind chimes, 36, 41, 46, 61, 64, 82, 90, 119, 126, 133, 151, 159, 169, 176
window boxes, 177, 179
windows, 119, 178–179
  inward and outward opening, 177
wood, 31, 172, 183
wood element, 8, 12–13, 14, 25, 54–59, 76, 79–80, 86, 126, 139, 142, 144, 154, 172, 173, 175, 186
  new year dates, 184–185
work stress, 180–181
work table, 30, 68–69, 104, 121, 122, 132–133, 161, 181
workplace, 14, 22, 30, 32–33, 50–51, 54, 66, 130–131
  compatibility, 137
  equipment, 69, 180–181
  low morale, 121, 180, 182–183

xiaoren, 124

yin and yang, 10–12, 29, 35, 38–39, 40, 50–51, 53, 54–56, 67, 75, 110, 139, 149, 158, 159, 170–171, 175, 178–183, 187
  symbols, 10, 17

Thunder Bay Press
An imprint of the Advantage Publishers Group
THUNDER BAY   5880 Oberlin Drive, San Diego, CA 92121-4794
P · R · E · S · S   www.thunderbaybooks.com

Copyright © text, illustrations, and design: Lansdowne Publishing Pty Ltd., 2003

ISBN 1-57145-996-0
Library of Congress Cataloging-in-Publication Data available on request.

Printed in Singapore by Tien Wah Press (Pte) Ltd

1 2 3 4 5   07 06 05 04 03